BETTER TO JOURNEY

This is a handful of cardamoms,
This is a handful of ghi;
This is millet and chillies and rice,
A supper for thee and me.
                    Rudyard Kipling.

BETTER TO JOURNEY

Travels Across the Roof of the World

MARGARET HOBBS

Foreword by Debbie Moore

A Deirdre McDonald Book
Bellew Publishing
London

To Susie and Helen for the laughter, fun, deep
friendship and immeasurable inspiration; and
for insisting that I write a book so that they could
read about their adventures – and wouldn't have
to keep a diary!

To John for being unerringly encouraging and
positive about everything, especially the book.

To Rhiannon, my good friend, who never lost
her enthusiasm, or patience, while she
deciphered the first HB version, the learning how
to type version and the stumbling into the
twentieth century version on a word processor.

To Pemba with gratitude, affection and respect.

And especially to my Mum – with love and
appreciation for everything.

First published in 1991
by Deirdre McDonald Books
Bellew Publishing Co. Ltd
7 Southampton Place, London WC1A 2DR

Copyright © Boddington Associates Ltd 1991

The right of Margaret Hobbs to be identified
as the author of this Work has been asserted
by her in accordance with the Copyright,
Designs & Patents Act 1988

Designed by Bob Vickers

ISBN 0 947792 63 5

Phototypset by Intype, London

Printed and bound in Great Britain by
Billing & Sons Ltd, Worcester

Contents

Foreword

S INCE much of my own professional life in the male bastions
of business has been spent encouraging women to realize their
ambitions – through fashion, dance and physical exercise – I find the
physical and mental achievements of these three women, Margaret
Hobbs, Susie Kaye and Helen Sadiq, featured so amusingly in this
book, impressive and I am delighted to contribute to such an enjoyable read.

I have known Helen for many years and I'm not surprised to
learn, in reading this book, that she, along with her companions,
found even more strengths to add to the list I knew she already had;
strengths which were stretched to the point of tears many times as
they travelled through the fabulous Himalayas hundreds of miles
away from civilization as we know it.

The story – told with a delightful sense of humour about such
horrendous happenings as monsoons, leeches, earthquakes, camping
in snow, gruelling walking for days up to 18,000 ft and seeing a
young porter, whom they'd grown to love, die – is an inspiration to
us all and an example of what can be achieved through perseverance.
For these women to have taken these previously undreamt of steps,
to Everest, K2, and Makalu base camp, where few women have
dared to tread, required the sort of courage most of us can only
aspire to.

They demonstrate clearly that you can get fit at any age, or
stage, of your life, that women can achieve tremendous objectives,
alongside being at home making the jam, if they want to, and that
when one has found the courage, as they did, the confidence comes
to tackle further ambitions, as Margaret did when she discovered
her skills as a writer. Her inspiration came to write about their
travels when she realized just how few women had been to K2 and
Makalu when they travelled there. Now armchair and real travellers
alike can immerse themselves in this lovely adventure story with its

vivid descriptions of rugged scenery and gentle mountain folk, or laugh out loud at the honest, unabashed humour of embarrassing moments highlighted by travelling al fresco with a band of male climbers.

It is the closely observed situations, and the self-effacing writing style, that make the book so human and eminently readable. I loved the characters drawn with such definition: Pemba with his kindness, Malcolm his impish charm, Doug Scott with his ability to face danger so coolly, Susie so caring, John so reliably strong, and Helen always wearing her earrings come hell or high water.

Margaret gives us a peep into the minds of international climbers faced with the anxieties of climbing K2 and Makalu; and she shows us her own overwhelming emotions, and those of her fellow trekkers, when fatigue gets too much. Her description of her near-death situation at the beginning also brings it home to us just how dangerous the thin atmosphere is at high altitude.

How many of us yearn to make such adventurous journeys, long to see the Himalayas, promise ourselves we'll go one day, I wonder? Most of us, I suspect, know that in the end we will lack the where-with-all to face the discomforts and privations to ever reap the rich rewards – but at least we can enjoy them now from the comfort of an armchair, or a beach, with no more effort required than having to turn the pages or reach for a glass of wine, which is just as well as you won't be able to put the book down; it's pure adventure, full of laughter, tears, pleasure and squirming horrors – and most of all true!

These women, and their friend John, endured it all to see three of the highest mountains in the world and fell in love with that mountainous land – and shining through all the grisly bits, the caring companionship, the insane and wonderful experiences, is the laughter ringing loud. And it is that laughter you'll share as you read their story. It's a definite understatement of considered achievements – and a must for everyone.

Debbie Moore,
Pineapple Dance Studios, London

Introduction

During our first trip – to Everest base camp – I kept a few sketchy notes in a pocket-sized notebook. It was hardly a diary, just jottings about things that amazed and amused us. Beyond that, this tatty little book had no significance at all other than as a personal *aide-mémoire*. Then, when we were stranded in Lukla for three days, I lost it. I was a bit disappointed, but, as I had no need of a detailed diary, it didn't worry me – till I started to write this book. It begins with Everest and naturally I thought I would need the diary, but to my surprise I didn't. I found that our first experience of the Himalayas had been such a bombardment of all senses that, three trips on, and three years later, I could recall every detail faithfully, even without the aid of my tatty little *mémoire*, but I've thought about the little notebook a lot!

Its loss highlighted how powerful the impressions had been and also underlined how radically my own expectations had altered. Altered, because at that time any idea of writing a book would have seemed quite fanciful, if not ludicrous. For any of us, for that matter, to write a book about our experiences was so far from our minds that we wouldn't have even dreamt about it. Now through having been to Everest, K2, and Makalu, and having written the book – all events originally way beyond my own expectations – I've seen that the most unlikely ideas are not ludicrous after all and that my perception has been considerably broadened. But still, it's amusing to reflect that it took the absence of a tatty little notebook for me to realize this.

Ours is not a story of great climbing courage, expertise and derring-do, nor is this a professional trekking guide or a travelogue. It is simply a tale of four friends and the sometimes amusing, sometimes extraordinary encounters we experienced trekking in the Himalayas. And although it's also a story of how we battled with our inner weaknesses and limited physical endurance, it's essentially a tale of fun laced with a bit of lip-trembling fear.

We made three excursions: one as a small independent group to Everest base camp in Nepal; the second as part of the support trek with the Anglo-American expedition on K2 in Pakistan's Karakoram range; the third, as part of a support trek again, this time with a British expedition to Makalu in Nepal. The latter expeditions were both led by Doug Scott, one of Britain's foremost mountaineers.

The three women were Susie Kaye, Helen Sadiq and myself. The fourth member of the group was our friend John Knowles. Helen and I had known John for eighteen years; we lived in the same Northamptonshire village. In the early years, John and his wife ran the village shop and all our children grew up together. Susie and I had been friends for nearly as long. I cooked her husband's breakfast for him on my honeymoon night! Between us, we have nine childr :n, and at the time of planning for Everest they were all, apart from Helen's youngest son, in their teens or early twenties.

The whole idea of trekking in the remote Himalayas had been John's. Helen, John and I were sitting in the Plough Inn at Upper Boddington one Sunday when John began expounding the delights of trekking in the lower terai regions of Nepal, since he had just come back from a week's exploratory trip. His great ambition though was to trek to Everest base camp – which is a bit further up!

Helen said that she had always wanted to see Asia, and I said that for twenty-five years I had dreamt, rather unhopefully, of going to India. 'Why don't you go with me then?' John said, and by the time the evening was over Helen and I had made up our minds to do just that.

Once we'd made the decision Helen and I found, rather to our surprise, that no reaction from our families, however shocked, could change it. It was as if the decision was set in stone, as if we really believed that it was our time to take off, even though no one else was interested in going with us – until a few weeks later when Susie heard. She was so excited by the idea that it was clear we were not going to be able to go without her, and it was her positive, ebullient enthusiasm that kept us from cancelling the idea, out of fear, many times. So now we were four and ready, in our minds, to set off.

The prospect of the journey besieged us with self-doubt, and further doubting questions from friends and family compounded the misgivings because we didn't have any convincing answers. 'Why do you want to spend a month cocooned in canvas on a mountain when the nearest thing to it any of you has tried is a marquee on the lawn at home? Why go up a mountain miles from anywhere when you have so much comfort at home? Why buy all this equipment – do all this training? Aren't you a bit old for all this? Don't you think it's a bit like starting at the top. Aren't you biting off a bit more than you can chew?'

Yes . . . but we were intractable; beyond dissuasion; and no note of scepticism would budge us. When we did examine our motives, it soon became clear that, having spent a large part of our lives holding up the ladder for the rest of our families, we felt it was our turn to see what was at the top – and step out for ourselves. There was a sense of urgency about going, a distinct feeling of the sands of time running out, and the desire to go grew till it arched over everything else.

A state of continuous excitement came over us. High on a buzz of adrenalin we began a fitness programme. Helen and I walked and walked, up to ten miles a day. John walked a little bit too, but he was already fit from hiking the Pennine Way, so he didn't need to walk the country lanes as Helen and I did. Susie didn't train at all. Apart from daily walking around London in her job as a nurse, which wasn't as far as it sounded she said, she'd walked around the round-pond at their house in Dorset – and that was it! But she worried about not having done as much as Helen and me and pleaded with us 'Not to keep walking so much. You'll be too fit and I won't be able to keep up.' However, we had no means of telling whether we'd be fit enough. We tried to gauge what 'normal fitness,' as it said in the trekking guides, was. Being able to walk ten miles a day, on tarmac roads at sea level, or being able to do John's mountainous bits, or would Susie's round the round-pond do? This went on for months, twelve, fourteen and we visited gyms and jogged and lost weight. We tweaked our knees, Helen hurt her back, and Susie broke her toe. At the appropriate intervals we got injected against every tropical disease known to man and a few more; when I visited my doctor one time for one of those expensive jabs, in an unguarded moment, I mentioned my knee. 'My dear,' he sighed with a doctor's typically long-suffering patience, 'the only time I see you in here is when you've sustained an injury – getting fit! Perhaps you shouldn't do so much?' Susie took care of the medical supplies and we all went to the dentist. We studied and bought the best equipment for trekkers, and all the best travel books on Nepal, and began the great read. In doing so we realized that, as we looked out over the landscapes of our lives, we'd all seen the same distant horizon beckoning and we felt a great need to explore it. We were fortunate, it came at a time right for us all to go together.

We are a good combination of friends, all different, and yet in so many ways alike. Helen is like a daffodil, jolly and bright with the promise of spring and sunshine in her laughter, but her feet are firmly rooted in the hard ground and she is well able to withstand the harsh winters of life should she have to. Her solid, warm input into her much-loved family, with three boys, has proved her strengths over and over again.

Susie is the original stout-hearted oak, strong, dependable, comforting and a positive statement that all things are possible in one's life. She proved that when she cured herself, homoeopathically, of lupus. She spreads her branches wide, over her family, patients, and many friends.

John is the leader, the inspiration. The one who cannot conceive of failure or doubt. The one who believes he can make anything happen and usually does. He works, caringly, at all manner of fundraising events, enthusiastically at travelling, and fanatically as nineth bat in the Boddington Cricket Club.

I just tag along, appreciating my good luck to have such fine friends; they talk a lot of common sense and I feed on their optimism.

Throughout our journeys our friendships survived and grew, and, happily, have been enriched by many new travelling companions. From time to time I've asked Helen and Susie why we go back on other treks? The same answer comes through clarion clear. The adventures, the stretching of ourselves personally – and the camaraderie. It's not just the climbers and trekkers with whom we've made such good friends, and who have helped us push ourselves beyond our imagination, but the Nepalese porters and *sirdars*, the Pembas, the Dorjees, the Ang Pananges and the Baltistani Nabis and Bhoms. Yes, there's also the lure of the wild, the lure of fascinating cultures and religions, and we are captivated by Kathmandu, but largely it is the people who make the memories endure – the reason why we go back.

Helen is now studying Buddhism and meditation and has trekked through Bhutan. She has sponsored five children: two Nepalese, two Indian and one Ethiopian. They write regularly to her and keep her up-to-date with their progress. They are all in fairly remote villages but one day we'd like to go and visit them.

Susie is studying the holistic approach to medicine and still practising her own immense healing powers. Her nursing confidence has grown measurably, and this year she has been asked to go with the Guardian Expedition to Mount El'brus in Russia, as one of the medical officers.

John never stops travelling the world or going up mountains, and having set up his own trekking company, he is busy researching new treks and leading others.

So now we have achieved a few ambitions, reached a few goals and had fun, presumably we don't need to go back. But, along with all the other discoveries we've made, we've learnt that once you have dared to venture into the most gloriously majestic fortress of the world, which lies like a crusty, sugar-coated necklace between the plains of India and the deserts of Tibet, thick with forests and incalculable numbers of flowers, you may never find a way out of its heart, or be free ever again of its charms. The people and the mountains have found their way into our hearts and we'll need to go back as soon as it's possible – and since we know now that anything is possible if you want it enough – it won't be long. Besides, after three trips we still haven't seen the fabulous rhododendrons of Nepal – in bloom!

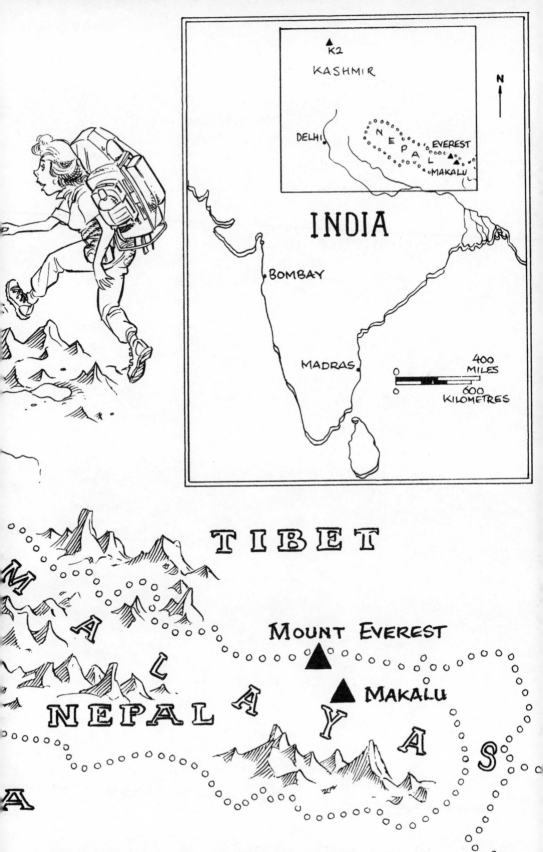

K2

KASHMIR

N

DELHI

NEPAL EVEREST

MAKALU

INDIA

BOMBAY

MADRAS

400 MILES

600 KILOMETRES

TIBET

MALAYAS

NEPAL

MOUNT EVEREST

MAKALU

A

PART ONE

KALA PATTAR △

MOUNT EVEREST
29,028 FT.
8,848 METR

GORAK SHEP

BASE CAMP

N

LOBUCHE

DUGHLA

PHERICHE

DINGBOCHE

PANGBOCHE

N E P A L

KHUMJUNG

TENGBOCHE MONASTERY

KHUNDE

NAMCHE BAZAAR

KATHMANDU

LUKLA AIRSTRIP

0   3   MILES

0   6   KILOMETRES

1

Better to Journey

NOVEMBER. It's early afternoon and the wind is blowing hard on the tent walls. Icy cold and dotted with snow, it drums on the canvas and gusts in through the flapping door. Snowflakes fall silently on my sleeping bag, melt into the warmed surface and leave dark stains. But since I am without the strength to lift myself up, cross the tent and struggle with the zip, the door will have to stay open. Canvas is poor protection against three feet of snow and twenty-five degrees of frost at 17,000 feet in the Himalayas, but lying here, ill and alone, I'm grateful even for that meagre comfort, and long for my friends to return.

Our tent is pitched, in a small snow-cleared patch, at Gorak Shep on the Khumbu Glacier. It's not the most convenient place to be ill, but for several hours now I've been lying here suffering from acute mountain sickness (AMS), and I'm frightened because I know that I could die from it if the right steps aren't taken.

Mountain or altitude sickness occurs, in some people, when the ascent is too rapid for the body to adjust to the decreased air pressure at high altitude. This makes it difficult for the lungs to draw in enough oxygen; generally only mild symptoms occur, such as head-aches, lassitude, nausea and sleeplessness. But in a more severe condition, however, fluids build up on the lungs and result in pulmonary oedema. Fluid may also build up on the brain, causing cerebral oedema, or they may both occur together. Mountain sick-ness can progress quite rapidly, coming on with very little warning, and to make the mistake of treating it without respect is foolhardy in the extreme. The only sure cure for it is to descend to an altitude at least a thousand feet lower as quickly as possible. This is something I will have to do – somehow – soon. The fluid has built up on my lungs and I should go down, but as I can hardly breathe, and am extremely weak, I don't know how I will be able to walk.

Yesterday our little party of five friends, Helen Sadiq, Susie Kaye,

John Knowles, Terry Mayer and myself – plus Pemba Norbu our Sherpa guide, two cook-boys, four porters and five yaks – trekked up here to Gorak Shep from Lobuche on the Everest trail. We had come to see the highest mountain in the world, Everest, Nepal's own jewel set in the mightiest crown on earth, the Himalayas.

It had been an eight day journey, and we'd made our last camp here, intending to set off for Everest base camp today. But when we arrived last night we'd found that Gorak Shep's only reference point, in the whole of the Himalayas, was a single, unoccupied, yak herder's hut, half buried in snow. It offered no balm for our tired bodies or flagging spirits and John had immediately got bad vibes about the place and declared it was 'the worst place in the world'. Now that I have fallen foul of altitude sickness, and lie here with only a sleeping bag between me and the frozen ground, I'm inclined to agree with him.

We had set out at 7.30 this morning, in thick mist, to walk up the last thousand feet to the base camp. It lies at the southern tip of the infamous Khumbu Glacier Ice Fall which flows in an ever-moving snarled mass of ice from the foot of Mount Everest. Pemba estimated that it would take four hours. The thin air made the walking hard but we pressed on steadily, drawing strength from our enthusiasm to reach our final goal. Then, only one hour out of camp, the sickness struck me – quite suddenly. It raged through my head, hammered in my chest and burnt through my lungs like a blowtorch. At first I plodded on, shambling behind the others, believing that if I rested frequently I could get there. I didn't want to give up now – not when we were only an ice field or so away. But my body thought differently and my heart threatened, with excruciating pain, to explode if I took another step. With no breath and no choice I had to concede, sadly, that this was the end of my aspirations – only one day away from Everest base camp.

The disappointment of falling at the last hurdle was immense, and having to watch my friends go on without me, almost unbearable. But there was nothing for it now but to get back to our bleak camp at Gorak Shep. It took me two and a half hours; taking a few steps at a time and resting on the rocks, I gulped in the air to ease the pains in my chest. Eventually I arrived back at the camp where I collapsed into the cold tent. That was seven hours ago now and since then I've been lying in a semi-conscious state, slipping in and out of colourful dreams, illusions and nightmares. The worst part, though, is being alone and the solitude terrifies me.

In a lucid moment it dawned on me that today is my birthday, and I couldn't help smiling at the irony of dying on that day. It also made me think poignantly about the bottle of champagne I'd carried up here so that we might celebrate the double header of my forty-fifth birthday and the success of getting to Everest base camp at 18,000 feet.

I certainly hadn't intended to spend this, of all days, in a sleeping bag. This was meant to be the high-water mark of our newly discovered pleasure: walking in the Himalayas. But now, I feel totally indifferent to both success and failure. The altitude sickness has given me a new perspective on the meaning of achievement and, as I lie here, incapable of going anywhere, I realize that just getting down the mountain and out of this alien environment would be a success that I could live with – quite literally.

All this rationale came to me after I'd been tortured by a horrible nightmare. In my dream a noise startled me. At first I thought it was my friends arriving back, but no one came and there was only silence. Then I heard it again: a faint rustling sound. My eyes darted towards the door, I felt nervous and vulnerable. What was it? Surely it was just the wind hitting the canvas, making it roll up and down in dark waves, making it snap angrily. Then I saw something out of the corner of my eye. Someone was there: a misty figure slithering dark and flat against the canvas. It loomed up over me for a second, twisted grotesquely in the shadows, and disappeared. The horror of it jolted me back to a trembling consciousness and, sweating with fear, I shrivelled down deep into my sleeping bag. Then, slowly, I looked around my little canvas shell. It had been my home now for eight days and I blinked at the familiar objects around me. Gradually they took on a comforting shape – Susie's bag, Helen's book, the Travel Scrabble – and as I recognized these friendly things, my mind eased a little, but my heart still raced on like a train.

Nightmares and I have never been strangers. I've always had them, but usually I endure the bad ones, with resigned equanimity, in the warmth of my own bed in more normal surroundings. Now, lying here in a tent miles from anywhere, shivering and alone in the dark, with no one to talk to, sick and hallucinating, I find them unendurable – and long for my friends.

Wryly, I reminded myself that in the first place I'd only wanted to go to India. That had been my original, longstanding, and burning ambition. Trekking had never been part of my earlier plans. What was I doing here anyway? Had our families been right when they pronounced us mad to want to come here at our age? What if the others didn't get back? What if I didn't ever get home? What about India? I consoled myself with the irrational thought that, if I didn't get back home, then at least I'd got closer to India than I'd ever done before.

As the time passed, I tried to recall how it had all begun. What had John said to us eighteen months ago in our local pub? The conversation filtered back, hazy, muddled.

'Hey Mags, would you like to go to Nepal?'

'Yes, I've always wanted to go to India. Ever since a friend at art school wrote her thesis on Asian art and the playing card.'

'Not India – Nepal,' he said, clicking his tongue and sighing deeply.

'Oh,' I said.

'Do you like walking?' he asked.

'Ye-s – but . . . ,' I answered cautiously, not quite sure what kind of walking he meant, and added, 'as long as it not uphill!'

He tutted again. 'Do you like camping?'

'I think so.' I shrugged. 'I don't know – I've never camped.'

'Well what about curry? I suppose you hate curry?' He seemed resigned.

'No,' I said defensively – and in the hope of getting something right, said, 'I like Helen's. Or a takeaway from the Star of Ruby or whatever it's called in Banbury. That's OK.'

'Oh Lord,' he groaned, hope gone, 'I s'pose you'll be all right.'

That, apparently, was how Helen, Susie and I had passed the would-be trekker's test. He had mentally ticked off the requirements, while we, with none of them, blithely agreed to do something about which we knew nothing. Now we are here, not studying the origins of the playing card in India, but trekking to Everest base camp in Nepal. I can hardly believe now that the trip originated in such a whimsical conversation, and as I lie here, perilously near to death, I can't help wondering how I ever let them talk me into it.

Nevertheless, for us three women (Helen, Susie and myself) half of the trip's appeal lay in the lure of adventure and a curiosity about the culture of Buddhism. The other half came from a burgeoning need to experience something outside our normally tidy, organized lives – before it was too late. We wanted something testing, something challenging, something more than the average pre-packed, hermetically sealed beach holiday we'd previously taken. John had presented us with the opportunity.

Admittedly, we are an unlikely trio for this kind of adventuring, all being in our mid- to late forties and all married, with teenage or adult children. The only exercise any of us had taken in years consisted of walking from the car to the curb, or skipping about in a jolly tennis game between a few large minted Pimm's. We'd never been more than a hundred yards away from a loo. Nor had we ever been away without our families – to whom walking to the foot of Everest seemed a preposterous thing to do. But we three, after much deliberation, decided to do just that. Why not? And because we had all been good friends for years – if one went, we all went. Then our friends and families, as we started training by walking between five and ten miles a day, began to treat the whole thing with a mixture of curious disbelief and a vocal scepticism about our ability to do it. This proved to be an irresistible bait, so that, eventually, we found ourselves revelling in the perverse pleasure of attempting to do something we'd been told we couldn't do.

Now John, he's different – though the same age. He's an enthusiastic sportsman, a great walker (a veteran of the Pennine Way and other walks), a would-be climber, a serious traveller and an ardent believer in the 'go-for-it' theory. Without him, his encouragement and great zest for life, we would never have dreamt of setting out to walk to the foot of Mount Everest.

Terry, the fifth member of the group is a friend of John's. He is also a keen walker, though this is his first trip to the Himalayas.

We women had thought, rather loftily perhaps, that somewhere along the line the mountains might reveal great truths and mysteries to us, that we might even discover something about ourselves. After many years of altruistic housewifery and mothering, we didn't really know what we truly liked any more, and though we were extremely apprehensive about what we perceived as the unknown, we decided to throw down the tea towel, hang up the rubber gloves and be off. And we certainly did learn something – something about mountains. We learnt that walking up to 18,000 feet is very hard work indeed.

In a perverse kind of way we'd liked it, pushing ourselves physically harder than ever before. We'd enjoyed testing our mental stamina and emotional fortitude and, so far, we'd endured the difficulties reasonably well. But here, today, for me, everything is different. All my resilience is gone and as I look at things through eyes clouded by a dangerous sickness I can be sure of only one thing: my own terrible fear.

It was nearly dark and the temperature was dropping rapidly when my companions crushed into the tent. They seemed tired but excited, and as the sea of faces bent down towards me I saw the glow of triumph in their eyes and knew they'd reached the base camp.

'You made it then,' I said, trying to control the quiver in my voice.

'Yes, we did,' they said gently, 'but how are you?'

'Pretty horrible,' I whimpered, pathetically near to tears, 'but better now that you're here. I can't tell you how glad I am to see you all.'

It was while we were talking about their day, as Susie held my hand, that I realized how much I *did* mind failing. And however much I tried to convince myself that it didn't matter, truthfully, in my heart I felt that it did. But this was not the time to indulge in disappointment, now was the time to believe that it was 'better to journey than to arrive.' I wondered if this is why we used these sayings: to soothe ourselves.

Susie, who is a part-time nurse, and had ministered caringly to all our ailments on the way up, engaged full nursing mode: thermometer in the mouth, fingers on the pulse and her eyes locked on the second hand as she timed the racing beats. She checked and rechecked till she was sure. Temperature 99.8, pulse 98, respiration 32, all rather high. During this brief medical examination she whispered with Pemba and John, in a voice low enough to make me nervous, but not loud enough for me to hear. I asked, in a wheezing voice, what they were saying.

'We were discussing the practicalities of taking you down to Periche tonight,' John said. 'Pemba says there's a hospital there.'

'Tonight – how?'

'On a yak!' Susie said. 'Pemba thinks we can get you down on a yak. You're pretty sick and I think we should go down.' She wasn't looking at me properly, and I searched urgently for her eyes, for reassurance that she didn't really mean what she'd just said. She looked at me, sensed my fear, and quickly continued, 'It's not wise for you to stay at this altitude – you know that.'

I did, but still couldn't believe what they were saying, and my head began to shake slowly from side to side, my body pressed defensively into the ground. 'No, no.'

'Now listen, Mags,' she said firmly, 'this is serious.'

I was still resolutely shaking my head, and fighting back the tears when she went on.

'It can be very dangerous – in a few hours – you know that.'

She spoke softly now, more persuasively. 'I really think we should. It'd be better to be cautious than . . . '

'Cautious!' I exclaimed weakly. 'I couldn't – I just couldn't – really, believe me.' And then, in desperation, with all the breath I could muster, I stated that nothing – absolutely nothing – would induce me to get on the back of a yak, and go down a treacherous mountain path in the dark. I breathed again deeply. 'I wouldn't ride a yak when I'm well – in the light – so I'm not going to ride one now in the dark, when I'm ill!'

She looked at me with the laser eyes of a concerned nurse. I cowered, terrified that she was going to insist, but felt I'd gained a little ground and then, to my enormous relief, she said, after an agonizing pause, 'Well, perhaps you'll be all right. You do seem to have some strength left, even if it is only to protest.' There was another, unnerving pause. 'After all, I don't think any of us relishes the idea of that journey in the dark. It could be a real case of the cure being worse than the disease,' she said, lightly. And with those words, after eight or nine hours, I began to feel some of the anxiety drain from my tired mind: I found the dread of the sickness paling beside the thought of riding on a yak, on a rocky path in the dark.

It was comforting to listen to the others bustling about the tent, and when Susie eventually shooed everyone off to bed, John turned back and said jokingly, 'So you don't think we'll be reading the last rites tonight then, gal.' I saw Susie shrug her shoulders and turn up her hands in an act of uncertainty. Then Pemba put his hands together, bowed his head a little, gazed with dark sombre eyes at us all, and said solemnly 'Namaste.' It means (among other things like Hello and Goodbye), may your God be with you!

I asked Susie if she had made radio contact with Mike Cheney (our trekking agent in Kathmandu) from base camp; a few nights ago she'd been very upset herself after she'd dreamt that her mother had died. Today she had especially wanted to get to base camp, to see if she could contact Mike in case he had any news. She told me that the Indian expedition had managed to get Mike on their radio, and that he hadn't heard anything from England. We hoped that this meant her fears were unfounded. Lack of communication with friends and family is quite difficult to cope with up here, and many times all of us would have given anything for a red telephone box to be just around the next rock so that we could put our minds at rest, and now we all understood her disquiet.

Following a lengthy discussion (because we were almost totally ignorant about altitude sickness) Susie decided on Diamox (a diuretic), antibiotics and paracetamol as treatment until they could get me down in the morning. The Diamox, we hoped, would drain some of the fluid from my lungs. This it seemed to do, and eventually I did feel more able to breathe, and even slept a little. Susie didn't. She lay awake, listening to me 'Cheyne-Stoking' (an intermittent breathing often heard prior to death). She, and Helen, kept a vigilant watch throughout the dark night, guarding me with the kind of care that bonds people together for life, a care for which I will be eternally grateful.

The following morning, 2 November, we willed that cold morning light to come up, with unprecedented fervour. Before dawn, John was up and gone to Kala Pattar, in a last, desperate attempt to see the south-west face of Everest and to take some photographs. Even though it was another 1,400 feet up, he thought that he could do it in a few hours and catch us up later, knowing that our progress down the mountain would be extremely slow and that Pemba had volunteered to carry me. We would go to the hospital in the village of Periche. It was 3,000 feet down to the village and he intended to carry me there, on his back!

Luckily, in the morning, getting dressed required no extra exertion for me as we hadn't taken off any of our clothes over the last few days. It was, indeed, more likely that we'd be putting extra ones on, if we had any, because the nights were so cold. We slept in six layers of clothes – thermal underwear, T-shirt, cotton shirt, sweater and a puffa vest, all under a large down jacket. At night we wore woolly hats or balaclavas and pulled our jacket hoods up over them.

Since we had left Kathmandu, the days had been sunny and bright, and particularly around midday we would peel off a layer or two while walking. The moment the sun disappeared behind the mountains, however, it became extremely cold and all the layers went straight back on again. Only the boots came off at night, and because they were wet they would freeze solid. So the efforts of Susie and Helen, trying to get these frozen lumps on to my feet, introduced a much-needed light note into what otherwise promised to be a fairly wretched day.

Helen and Terry decided that they should go on with the cook-boys to establish the camp and warn the hospital to expect us. Pemba, Susie and I would get there as soon as we could. Pemba explained that some Americans were camped about a quarter of a mile away and he wanted us to go there and wait for him while he broke camp, loaded the yaks and got the cook-boys away. He felt we would be more comfortable. But I looked with a sinking heart at the imperceptible slope of the path to their camp, thinking that this, to me, could prove to be the steepest hill of all. Certainly it proved to be a painful lesson in the dangers of altitude.

How we struggled, Susie and I, crawling like snails up the slight incline towards the American camp! We resembled a *bria* (Nepalese idiom for old woman) and her nurse. I was leaning heavily on a walking stick, stepping, stopping, panting in pain and anguish; the nurse was continually encouraging the patient with reassuring words. But self-preservation is a powerful force, and it gave me the modicum of strength that I needed for a short time, until, totally distressed, utterly spent and in severe pain, we reached the camp. I slumped on to a rocky bank.

While Susie was watching over me, a nauseatingly healthy young man strolled over. He told us, quietly in an American accent, that he was a doctor. We were considerably heartened at this good news.

'I wondered if I could help with anything?' he said, pausing carefully, 'because, if you don't mind me saying so, you don't look good.'

This simple, sympathetic observation, stole any slender hold I might still have had on my emotions, and I burst into tears. Practical efficiency I can cope with when I'm feeling frail and feeble, but not sympathy. That will reduce me to tears in a heartbeat, and I cried and cried.

Susie explained to the American that we were fortunate to have Pemba taking care of things and listened as he expressed some concern about a woman in their own group, who was also suffering from altitude sickness. They needed to get her down as quickly as possible, he said. Her co-ordination was deteriorating rapidly and she'd gone into a coma. The problem was that she was very tall and heavy, and much larger than the average Nepalese man (about five foot four inches), and so none of their Sherpas (however willing) could possibly carry her.

'Hers sounds like cerebral oedema, doesn't it?' Susie whispered between her teeth as the doctor walked away, having made us promise to call him if we needed his help. 'Thank goodness yours is only on the lungs,' she added, to which I gave the faintest smile. It was cold comfort but I new knew what she meant, and now, feeling concern for the American woman served to distract us both a little from my sickness, although we were still extremely apprehensive about our journey down.

In the mountains in Nepal everything is carried on the back, by man, woman, child or beast. A rope, called a *tumpline*, made out of yak hair, is laid across the forehead and falls down the back. A *doko*, or conically shaped basket, in which the load is carried, is tied to the *tumpline*, and the weight is taken by the forehead and the neck muscles. It looks painful but the advantage of this method is that it leaves the arms free and allows the use of a sturdy stick. In this way the Nepalese carry loads of anything up to a hundred pounds, or more, and will even carry over their own body weight. Just looking at this method is enough to bring on a migraine in a mechanized Westerner, but in the mountains of Nepal it is the norm and it was how Pemba intended to carry me.

He took off his Harris Tweed cap (no doubt a gift from a climber), folded it double and put it between the abrasive yak-hair strap and his forehead. Then, resting a piece of wood in the cradle part of the sling behind his back, he stooped down and motioned me to sit in it. Bewildered but willing, I struggled into the little seat. With my arms around his neck and legs round his waist, he used his trusty staff and powerful leg muscles to lever himself up, with me, a similar body weight, on his bent back.

Susie looked on in amazed admiration and inquired if he was all right. He patted his slightly rounded little tummy, assured her that he was and said that he needed the exercise! He must have flashed her a huge grin, as I could see it reflected in Susie's smile. In this way, we set off down the narrow mountain path.

Whoever coined the phrase 'grace in the face of adversity' might have been talking about Pemba. Not only did he demonstrate the legendary Sherpa courage and fortitude needed to carry out this Herculean task, but he was also a constant inspiration to us with his dignity, charm and humour. I felt totally safe on his broad back, redolent of the evocative wood-smoke which pervades all the Nepalese people, and something herbal in his hair. Even in the most difficult situations, like negotiating slippery boulders in fast-flowing streams, or picking his way through rocks and boulders on steep downward paths, he was as sure-footed as a mountain goat, and our confidence in his determination to see the job through never wavered.

It took us nearly nine hours to do what would normally have been a five-hour walk, and it was dark when we finished. We stopped many times for Pemba to rest and take the strain off his back and forehead. Throughout the day he would look for a suitably positioned rock, back up to it, and drop me off like a sack of potatoes, which is just about how I felt. But the more we lost altitude, and the more alert I became, the more conscious I grew of the strain and discomfort I was causing him. I began to make embarrassed apologies when we stopped, but he dismissed them with an emphatic nod of his head and an enviable smile that seemed to come from the bottom of his heart.

Susie stayed at Pemba's heels, always ready with drinks from the water bottle, glucose tablets, vitamin tablets and any other available refreshment. Pemba also had his own supply of tinned pineapple chunks. Apparently these are his favourite food and he carried them in a bag on his chest. He would sit on a rock – handsome, compact, and immaculate, with a face the colour of a burnished chestnut, warm jet-black eyes, and excellent teeth (unusual up here) – and open a tin with his Swiss army knife. He chewed up the chunks, drained the juice and wiped his mouth on the back of his hand; but he never stopped long, just long enough to eat the pineapple, and then we'd be off again. We made steady progress, often having to climb a long way up to go down, acting out the required snakes and ladders of mountain walking. The relief we felt when we first saw the distant village of Periche was truly memorable.

We arrived at the floor of a wide, flat valley and in the dusk we could see pinpoints of flickering light from the houses surrounded by a gossamer mist. Sure that our traumatic little odyssey was coming to an end, with our hero struggling triumphantly in, we pressed on, fired with new enthusiasm and anxious to close this horrible chapter of our trip. 'Nearly there now,' Susie said, as we watched what we thought were the lights getting closer. But we were wrong. An hour passed by and the tiny, butter-oil lights didn't come closer. It was like a mirage. The more we walked, the more elusive the village seemed – and the more worried we became. Eventually, we realized, somewhat despondently, that the crystal-clear mountain atmosphere had completely fooled us and that the village was still a very long way off. Our resolve began to dwindle and we grew increasingly concerned about Pemba's strength. But he did just what he had done all day, pressed steadily on carrying me with him. To Susie and me it felt like a cruel epitaph to an already harrowing day, but we kept our eyes on the little beacons, willing them nearer, for what seemed like an eternity. Then suddenly, stepping out of the dusky mist, like Pip's convict on Romney Marsh, we saw John and the cook-boys laughing, smiling, calling and we were overjoyed.

The lads congratulated our deserving Pemba by boisterously slapping him on the shoulder, affectionately ruffling his hair and joking with him. We laughed feebly, exhausted. John had caught us up earlier, just as we expected, and had gone on to bring help back. Now Ang Panang (one of our cook-boys) insisted on taking over Pemba's work and I was transferred on to his back. Although the drop in the altitude had had its desired effect, and I was able to breathe more normally, I still couldn't have walked that last half mile. Ang Panang trotted along, shouting back and forth in fun, and soon we arrived at the village where Helen and Terry were waiting.

How conditioned we are by words! I was so surprised to see that Periche was only a handful of houses, because the word 'hospital' had given me the idea of something much larger. I had visualized its setting as more than just a hamlet with a few one-roomed wooden houses and a hotel built of jerry cans. Pemba's 'hospital' was in fact a Trekkers' Aid Post with two rooms; a surgery with a warming log-burning stove, the other a bedroom.

The post had an American lady doctor. To our surprise, she said, in no uncertain terms, that she 'had no sympathy at all for rash, irresponsible adventurers who came up into these remote mountain regions and charged up to 18,000 feet too quickly for their bodies to adjust to the altitude, because they were either too casual about the dangers of the mountains, or just didn't care, and then caused havoc, when they inevitably got ill, by expecting help which neither she, nor anyone else, could give.' We reeled back, not really having thought about ourselves in this way, and felt extremely embarrassed. Pemba looked scared stiff. Her eyes bored unflinchingly into ours and after a cold pause she questioned us, accusingly, about another sick woman, whom she'd heard was being brought down here today – what did we know about that? The icicles hung off her words – and froze our replies. We denied certain knowledge, pretended we didn't know. But she didn't believe us. She'd heard it all before. She was tired of it and, seeing us wriggle on the hook, became even more contemptuous of frivolous trekkers.

So there we were, after this horrendous day, huddled around the stove in this dear little surgery in which we'd hoped to find succour, flinching under the verbal blows of an overworked doctor, while she, with her long hair, flowing ethnic dress and fingerless gloves, continued to berate us and to put me through a test similar to that used for drunks at the police station, pre-breathalyser. I performed the tests with due contrition, afraid to do anything else.

'Can you walk straight along this painted white line? Yes, OK. Touch your nose with the forefinger on your right hand. OK. Now with your left hand. Bend your head back and let me look in your eyes. You look all right to me, go home and rest. Look, you got away with it this time, but never take altitude lightly again. Our work here is with the mountain people, and we don't have the oxygen or the drugs or the facilities for reckless . . . '

John interrupted with apologies, and offered a donation to her medical funds. The diplomacy paid off, and almost immediately the doctor relaxed, much to Susie's relief, because she was interested in the doctor's work and wanted to talk to her about it. She learnt, to her delight, that she had done the right thing in administering Diamox, and the doctor was just telling us that the hospital was mostly funded by Japanese and American money and that she was there for eighteen months doing voluntary service, studying the health problems of the Nepalese, when the door swung open. The sound of people shouting and scuffling about outside flowed into the tiny room and a young porter followed by a trekker burst through the door.

'Very sick, very sick,' the porter said, gesticulating wildly back out towards the darkness and, waving at the doctor to come on, he rushed out again. It was the American lady! Our heads snapped round to the doctor, filled with unease about what would come next. We watched her. Did we detect the slightest roll of the eyes, catch the merest intake of exasperated breath, see her shoulders slump at the tiresome news? I thought so, and couldn't help feeling bad. But I was riveted by the drama in this remote little surgery, until suddenly I felt strong hands under my arms – John and Susie – propelling me firmly towards the door. 'Come on, you, we're leaving,' they insisted, and before anyone could even so much as say 'altitude sickness' they'd half lifted me through the door, and out into the black night, with Helen, Terry and Pemba hard on our heels. 'It's time you were in bed,' they said. 'You're supposed to be ill – and we've all had just about enough of you for one day!'

2

A Baptism by Fire

IN the morning, we decided to stay at Periche for the day. We all needed a rest, as everyone was feeling some ill effects from the thin air. I was much improved, and although I was still extremely weak and had no appetite, I dearly wanted to walk down the mountain, tomorrow, under my own steam.

So Helen and I lay in our tent long into the morning; Helen was quite unashamedly sybaritic about lying in her sleeping bag because she suffered from the cold more than the rest of us. She also got very tired by the end of the day and the warning signs of this exertion were what we referred to as 'the dreaded pursed lips.' It meant that she needed warmth and rest. All the way up she had amused us by stating that immediately after the boys had put up the tent, she, unlike Captain Oates, would be 'going inside and would *definitely* be some time'. She'd scramble hurriedly into her sleeping bag, sigh deeply as if paradise had been regained, and firmly slide up the zip. Helen has always been known affectionately by her close friends as 'Hen' or the 'the poire belle Hélène', but this new hibernating instinct inspired yet another nickname and we called her 'Helena Horizontalis', which obviously appealed to her enormous sense of humour. She knew it bore no reflection on her mental strengths, as tenacity ought to have been her middle name. Her physique also belied her strength and was heavily disguised by baby fine, fair curly hair, the palest of complexions and a slight frame. But we didn't make the mistake of equating her physical fineness with a lack of backbone, and she almost daily surprised us with her bulldogish attitude to keeping going when she was clearly worn out. It was, I'm sure in part, due to her undying sense of humour; she could always see the funny side of things even in the worst situations.

As I lay there thinking about Pemba, I asked Helen if she remembered when we first saw him.

'In the Shangrila Hotel, do you mean?'

'No, before that. We saw him running along the road, in Kathmandu, didn't we?'

'Did we?'

'Yes, we were riding the bicycle rickshaw home in that wide avenue. Was it King's Road? The one where the Banyan trees were dripping in fruit bats, do you remember?'

'Ugh! Yes, don't remind me.'

'This man came running past us when we were stopped in the traffic, remember that? Then we passed him. And when we'd stopped again, he came floating by again, still running effortlessly. I thought about him then. Not just how quickly he'd covered the ground – nor how much more efficient than the rickshaw he was – but how he ran with such ease in all that heat. I was amazed. Then later, when we were having lunch in the garden, who should walk over to join us but "the running man" and Mike told us he was our Sirdar! I felt I already knew him then, and we liked him right away, didn't we? He had such a lovely smile. Of course, being a hill man and not a town wallah was the reason he could run so easily. All that extra oxygen down there, compared with living up in the mountains, would make running in Kathmandu very easy for him, wouldn't it?' I paused now that I was transported back to Kathmandu. 'He must feel light as a feather, all floaty like a bird down there.' I droned on, when suddenly it struck me that that was what Helen would like, to be back in Kathmandu, in the garden of the Shangrila Hotel. I told her.

'Oh yes,' she agreed. 'With a drinker wallah bringing me a large G and T or two.'

For a moment we both dreamed of lush lawns, English roses, tropical plants and fountains, all being tended to, every day, by an army of silent gardeners – it was a dreamy sort of garden, in a time warp from the days of the Raj.

'Talking of that, Mags, what about the champagne? When are we going to drink it?'

I laughed, knowing that the half-bottle of gin that she'd brought with her was nearly empty. I knew that because I'd helped her drink it. It was purely for medicinal purposes of course, and each night we would just have a capful to ease aches and pains.

'Good question,' I said, thinking about it. 'Well, I'll tell you what, we'll wait now till I'm better and then we'll have another birthday.'

'What do you mean? You'll have two birthdays – like the Queen?'

'Yes, I think so,' I said, cheered by the idea. 'I didn't care much for the first one, did you? It wouldn't require much effort to improve on it, would it?'

'Phew! I shouldn't think so, the first one couldn't have been much worse – for you particularly,' she sympathized.

'Somewhere nice on the way down,' I said, and cast my mind back to the route we'd taken coming up, and as I searched my memory, all the events of the previous eight days came crowding back into my mind.

We'd left the Shangrila Hotel in exotic Kathmandu on 24 October and, like so many who had gone before us, took our lives in our hands and flew in an ancient Fokker Friendship to Lukla. Landing on its short take-off and landing (STOL) airstrip is possibly one of the most hair-raising flying experiences in the world. The 'runway' lies at a 120-degree angle, 9,315 feet up on a small plateau in the Khumbu Himal. They say the uphill slope slows down the landing, whereas the downhill one, which ends abruptly at a cliff edge, speeds up the takeoff. It was built in 1965 to help service the hospital and school-building in Khunde, which was instigated by Sir Edmund Hillary.

When we first arrived in Kathmandu, John had been terribly excited because he had spotted Sir Edmund Hillary at the airport, but he made us a little apprehensive when he reminded us that Hillary's wife and daughter had been killed on this flight up to Lukla. Bad weather moves around quickly in the mountains, and sometimes these little planes lose their way. 'There are rocks in the clouds up here,' the pilots jest.

Fortunately for us, we didn't have any bad weather during the forty-minute flight, and the first day of walking, from Lukla down to Phadking at 8,700 feet, by the river, had been especially easy and pleasant, even though the effects of the altitude were already evident. We'd camped beside the raging Dudh Kosi (milk) river, which is aptly named as it is white with glacial scree from the foot of Mount Everest. But on the second day, to Namche Bazaar, at 11,283 feet, we'd found that the rains had washed away not only houses and bridges, and had cut the village off for some weeks, but it had also washed away most of the path from the river. Our itinerary had read 'Second day: trek to Namche Bazaar, depending on state of new trail (result of flash floods)' and we hadn't really understood what that meant, but we soon did. The old path, which had been gentler and circuitous, had slipped down the hillside in great chunks and the locals had hacked out a new one. The crucial difference being that the new one was cut, 'temporarily,' Pemba said, almost straight up the 2,600 feet!

We'd left England only a few days before (where we'd been training for months), and were horrified to find that we were poorly prepared for that relentless, almost vertical climb on the second day. It had nearly crippled us: a real baptism by fire! Willpower alone had dragged us up that hill, and we had been filled with the nagging doubt that our enthusiasm might have wildly outstripped our ability. The only encouraging moment had come when, late in the afternoon, Pemba's young daughter had come trotting down the mountain path from the village, holding her baby brother by the hand. Although Pemba wasn't as overtly pleased to see his daughter (unlike his son, who being a boy, was the more precious child), we were thrilled. We could have hugged her, if we'd had the strength, because we knew that she couldn't have come far with such a small toddler. She was like a land bird spotted at sea, and she lifted our spirits enormously. We'd slept well that night.

In the morning John came to the tent and insisted that we get out of bed and see what we'd come all this way to see. We stood agog at the village of Namche Bazaar. It was set in a natural amphitheatre at the head of a plateau which was high above the river, circled by snow-capped mountains and the bluest sky. Black-and-white timbered buildings clung to the sloping, south-facing walls of the bowl, and windows sparkled in the morning sun. A stream flowed down through the village, and gurgled past a huge *chorten* (sacred statue of Buddha), which was painted in bright colours and bedecked, from its top to the ground, with prayer flags blowing in the breeze. It was a spectacular sight and we revelled in it.

We spent that day scrutinizing every detail of the important village, which is the commercial hub of the Khumbu District, which has only two other neighbouring villages. There salt, silk, wool, chickens, grain, rice, tea and many other staples had been traded from China and Tibet to India, in a manner unchanged, for thousands of years. Although everything was inexpensive by our standards, we still acted out the required bargaining when we bought numerous pieces of hand-crafted silver jewellery and lengths of hand-woven cloth. We mingled with the women at the stream and watched curiously as they washed themselves, their babies, their pots and clothes, and gathered their drinking water, all in the same part of the stream from which the animals drank. We lunched in the camp under the *chorten*, and Pemba served the meal on a little table covered in a red-checked cloth. We took tea at his mother's house and supper in a restaurant, where we sampled the Indian beer. It was our first experience of a Nepalese village and we were thrilled by it all.

At that stage there were six of us: Susie, Helen, John, Terry, myself – and Richard, another friend of John's. But later that night we'd been profoundly shocked when Richard announced that he was going home! He said that he wasn't feeling well, that he was homesick, and that he had definitely made up his mind to go down in the morning, and back to England. This after only two days was something of a bombshell, and we couldn't understand it. Especially as he was much younger and fitter than the rest of us. We'd been preparing for the trip for twelve months and knew that he, in particular, had been tremendously excited about coming.

It had a strange and unsettling effect on us. Probably because we were all a little bit nervous of the unknown ahead, and Richard's decision seemed to remove part of the psychological prop that we thought we needed. We worried about having failed him, or wondered if he'd sensed something ominous ahead, but if he did, he didn't say so. It had been the second reminder, in twenty-four hours, of how vulnerable we were and how easily we could be unsettled in these remote regions.

The next morning Pemba arranged for one of the porters to take Richard back to Lukla. We gave him messages to take home and bade him a confused farewell.

The rest of the journey through the mountainous Sagarmatha National Park (Sagarmartha is the official Nepalese name for Mount Everest but the locals call it Chomolungma, Mother Goddess of the World) was a series of enlightening and stimulating encounters. We'd been continually awed by the beautiful Himalayan ranges and peaks, especially Ama Dablan (22,493ft), the quintessential snow-capped mountain, and amazed by the infinite variety of flora and fauna; strong, towering oaks, blue pines and sixty-foot-high rampant rhododendron trees, down to tiny blue gentians and pale, delicate violets. We'd even had the occasional glimpse of the timid muntjac deer, and been enchanted by the cheeky grey squirrels and the impeyan pheasant, which is sometimes called the rainbow pheasant because of its nine colours. It is the national bird of Nepal. We'd spotted the hen-birds sometimes cleverly camouflaged under the

juniper, or sage bushes, while the edelweiss, and the purple colum-
bine had seemed to prefer a sunny, open spot on the rocky outcrops.
Everything had been a delight, and the whole rich mosaic of the
Khumbu region had more than fulfilled our expectations.

A day's walk from Namche Bazaar brought us to the sacred
Buddhist monastery, Thyangboche, at 12,687 feet. Here, we'd been
fortunate enough to witness the most holy of their religious cere-
monies, the Mani Rindu, presided over by the Lama, or head monk
of the district. It lasted two days, and we watched the monks perform
their sacred dances, symbolically driving out evil spirits, while they
pledged themselves to the untiring search for truth, self-effacement
and purity through the renunciation of all worldly possessions. Cym-
bals clashed and small brass bells tinkled as the fourteen-foot-long
horns hummed out the long, deep, eerie sound which is peculiar to
these parts of northern Nepal and originates in Tibet. Villagers walk
for ten days to prostrate themselves to the Lama, who, as head of
a district, was second in importance only to the Dalai Lama. He
was attended by novice monks and entertained with ritual tea drinking. The villagers sat with their blankets swept around their
shoulders, and as they laughed at the clowns and jesters, they
coughed continuously in the cold air. It was there that I'd first
noticed the chronic coughing and realized that it was endemic to
the mountain people. It is very alarming until you get used to it,
especially as they all seem to suffer from it. They also suffer miserably from goitres, a swelling of the thyroid gland due to the lack of
iodine in the water.

We turned the Buddhist prayer wheels, walked to the left of the
Mani walls built of engraved gravestones, and watched the billowing
prayer flags, torn by the wind, carry the people's prayers to the gods.
In the daytime the white flags stood out against sunny blue skies;
at night they were lit by a dazzling moon and framed by the biggest,
brightest stars imaginable, and when we lay quietly, tucked up in
our sleeping bags, the haunting clang of yak bells lulled us off to
sleep. We travelled through the hamlets of Dingboche and Lobuche
and crossed swinging rope bridges, which terrified me. We drank
tea at the tea houses and ate potatoes cooked in the ashes of the fire
while Pemba gleaned mountain gossip from the lodgekeepers. Often
we spoke of the trust and hospitality that we'd received at the
Thyangboche tea house, where the toothless, illiterate, cheerful old
cook had motioned us to write down what we'd eaten, add up our
own bill, and pay what we thought we owed!

At night in the tent with Susie, we read and reread the scant but cogent pieces of medical advice contained in a leaflet about the dangers of altitude sickness. But nevertheless, we completely ignored the obvious signs: the headaches. And this, despite the fact that some of us, me in particular, had been suffering badly from them for days. We didn't realize that they were an early-warning sign of sickness. Headaches, breathlessness and loss of appetite are all rather ambiguous ailments and could be easily attributed to exertion or to the unfamiliar diet which brings on diarrhoea and bedevils every traveller here. We just took whatever pills we thought necessary and pressed on.

We did heed, however, some of the wise porters we'd met on the trail as we laboured up to 17,000 feet, because we had to. They warned us, as Pemba did, to 'step and rest, step and rest, and when you think you're going as slowly as you can – go slower.' Later we learned that it was the best prescription for warding off altitude sickness; but we foolish Westerners measure 'slow' by a different yardstick, and didn't take their advice seriously enough. So although we had a wonderful experience, coming up, we'd also been blind to the perils of the altitude and had not noticed that our little cup of joy was close to overflowing.

Back in the present, Helen's voice interrupted my reflections, bringing me back to the tent at Periche. She was talking about the luminous blue ice pinnacles they'd seen on the way up to base camp and how an Indian Army captain had given them much-missed things like bananas, nuts and chocolate for tea. She was telling me about radioing down to Kathmandu for Susie when I asked her to tell me about Everest. How did it look close up?

'How did it look?' she repeated with surprise. 'I don't know, we didn't see it! Well, only just a bit – and I couldn't make it out anyway among all the other peaks – so I don't think I've seen it yet!' She was rather casual about this and yawned deeply.

'What do you mean?'

'Well, you can't see it very well, from base camp,' She yawned again.

I was speechless, wondering how I'd missed this vital piece of information.

'That's why John had to go up to Kala Pattar', she continued, 'to see Everest and to get the photographs. Why do you think he left us – on that day of all days? Because that's where you really see – '. Her explanation was cut short by the dull throb of a helicopter.

There's a lot of helicopter movement between here and base camp, as the Indian Army had an expedition on Everest, and so we were quite used to hearing them buzz around. This one, however, didn't sound as if it were going past. It sounded very close. In fact it sounded as if it were about to land on the tent!

3

A Fistful of Dollars

HELEN put her head out of the tent, searching for the helicopter. 'I can't see it,' she said. 'It must be right behind the wall.'

'Shall we go and see?' I asked. 'I wouldn't mind a little walk – test the legs – what do you think?' I thought I wouldn't get her out of bed, but she readily agreed and reached for her jacket.

We emerged into the bright sunlight to see an army helicopter behind us, not a hundred yards away from the medical post. We walked slowly, and I was pleased to find that all the pain had gone from my chest. That at least boded well for tomorrow. A tight knot of people, including Susie, John and Terry, were gathered around the pilot and his mate. We closed in on the group, and were surprised to hear the doctor in a heated discussion with the pilot. Susie, standing at the edge of the group, explained that the doctor had asked the pilot to take the sick American woman down to Kathmandu, and she had been shocked to hear the doctor say that the woman might die in a couple of hours if she weren't given oxygen. But the pilot was refusing. We moved in close and heard him say that he was allowed to carry only army personnel and since he was going up to base camp to pick up injured soldiers he wouldn't have room for any other passengers, however ill they might be. His gaze shifted awkwardly from the floor to the doctor's face or cast about our group for support. But there wasn't any; no one could sympathize with him and his callous refusal. The doctor was pleading, but he remained unmoved, arguing that his duties lay elsewhere, and that this mess was not of his making. His flint-hearted inflexibility left us with a sour taste, and we realized that this was a dire warning of our own fragile position.

The crew coldly boarded the helicopter. At first we ducked away from the blast of its propellers, but as it lifted up and turned away we saw it was marked with the red cross. We watched it fade mockingly into the sky!

Someone said that the doctor had given the American woman oxygen for twenty minutes last night, from the post's solitary bottle, but that she would need at least two hours' oxygen to save her life. Now we couldn't help sympathizing with the doctor. She was faced with an invidious decision between draining her own essential supplies, knowing it would take months to get a replacement bottle, and trying to get the patient to a lower altitude. This could, in any case, take too long, and to be taunted with the possibility of the army helicopter was cruel indeed. She concluded that she couldn't help with her limited supplies, and advised the Americans to take the patient (now comatose) down the mountain straight away. As there was no other means of transport, the patient would have to be taken by yak.

Now yaks don't like people and are acknowledged, even by their greatest champions, to be irascible animals at the best of times. We'd seen an example of this ourselves, only a few days previously, when, without thinking, a trekker had moved to the outside of a narrow path to let a yak pass on the inside of him. Although proximity had been the yak's only provocation, it had lowered its huge horns and charged the man. He stepped back, lost his balance and fell over the edge of the cliff. Fortunately, a spiky thorn bush about fifty feet down broke his fall, and the hapless fellow clawed his way back up the cliff with just a few scratches. He was very shocked – and lucky. A yak's reaction to a sick rider was not difficult to predict.

The Americans nevertheless hired a beast, typically fiery-eyed, and set about trying to lift the insensible woman on to its back. It snorted, bucked and shook its head wildly. A young boy tried to calm it and held on to a rope around its neck. Eventually, they succeeded in getting the big, comatose woman on to the animal's back. She lay slumped forward over its neck, slipping from side to side, and would have fallen off had her friends not held her on. This pathetic little group of worried people then inched its way across the grass and out of the village. How that wide load could possibly negotiate the narrow downward trail safely was incomprehensible to us; it was impossible not to be concerned for them. We reflected that the group might easily have been us – if it hadn't been for Pemba.

He was preparing lunch when we got back to the tents, boiling up the daily diet of potatoes, making chapattis and brewing the tea – *chi*, as it's called in Nepal – which had become the mainstay of our strength. Susie was unable to bear it made with the excessive amounts of sugar and yak butter so favoured by the Nepalese, and drank it black – to Pemba's amazement. But we needed its cheering effects each day, and drank as much as we could.

We were just pondering the chances of getting our favourite tinned tuna for lunch when we heard the helicopter coming back. It swooped around the village and, hovering over the same unmarked landing pad, tentatively squared up the skids to the ground and then settled down. The whirling propellers spun from a barely visible blur to four thick paddles, and then, in slow motion, flopped over. Curiosity got the better of us and we hurried back, hard on the heels of the doctor and the other trekkers.

The doctor was clearly heartened by the news that they had come back to pick up the woman and take her to Kathmandu. The pilot said he would wait if someone went to fetch her. A runner was hastily dispatched and, threading his way through the small gathering, set off at an easy trot to bring the group back. Our spirits were greatly lifted; at least the woman now had a chance, we felt. Then came the rub: the pilot said they would have to be paid before they took the woman down.

'Of course,' the doctor said.

'In dollars. Cash!' the pilot added quickly.

'Yes, yes, I understand. How much would it be?' she asked briskly, innocently.

'Three thousand dollars,' he replied shiftily.

It stunned her. For a minute she couldn't speak. Her jaw hung open. When she did it was to loose a tirade of scorn. He blustered back, and if the conversation earlier had been heated, then it could only be said that, now, this avaricious figure ignited a positive blaze of indignation. People pitched in from all sides, urging him to be reasonable, to be realistic, telling him that nobody had that kind of money and asking why the Indian Army should demand so much. But the pilot was intractable.

The doctor was struggling, trying to reason with him, but she was beginning to reach the end of her patience. Then John tried. He needed to tread warily through this minefield of emotion. It was important not to blow the only rescue possibility they had, and he asked if they would take any other currency. John told them that we could raise more if they would accept sterling as well as dollars.

'What about travellers' cheques?'

'No, nothing but dollars. Only cash,' the pilot stated in the now familiar, pitiless tone, 'only dollars.'

John, whose heart lay in the mountains and trekking, is also a successful businessman, and was well used to negotiating hard bargains. He pressed on. Three thousand dollars was impossible; nobody carried large amounts of cash on a trek. He pointed out that we in particular had been encouraged to leave most of our money (and our passports for that matter) in the trekking agent's safe in Kathmandu. It was likely that everyone here had done the same thing. Would they take whatever we could raise between us?'

We girls had begun to speculate as to how they'd arrived at such an inflated figure; perhaps they'd radioed down to headquarters or they had decided, up at the base camp, to leave one of the injured men there, and share whatever spoils they could get from us. It seemed likely that this figure allowed someone to cream off a substantial amount of cash.

Gradually the mood cooled. They seemed to be reassessing the situation. There was a long uncomfortable silence. Perhaps they were considering what they could get. We waited, apprehensive, tense. Then the pilot shrugged his shoulders and asked grudgingly, 'How much do you have?' Immediately we delved into our money belts, rucksacks and pockets, pulling out everything we had. The Americans produced the most promising-looking wads, and John counted the resulting amount. We all nervously counted it with him.

'Six hundred dollars.' He proffered the money. Would they accept it? We stood like stone statues, not daring to breathe. Then, with a slight acquiescent shrug, the pilot's embarrassed eyes briefly met John's, and he reached out his hand. John thrust the fistful of dollars into it — and we all breathed normally again.

The folly of not carrying money when cash carries the clout was the lesson we'd just learnt, but it also posed a perturbing question. Are we wealthier Westerners responsible for this money-grasping coldness? Is this our teaching? I would hate to think so and hope not. Perhaps a more profound truth lies in the fact that ever since time began man has required his pound of flesh — anywhere in the world.

It was a solemn, troubled little procession that retraced its steps towards the helicopter. They hadn't gone far, but all hope seemed to have left them. Even the good news of the crew's change of plan didn't seem to have brought much joy either. Possibly it was clouded by the fear that it might be too late. Susie and John helped as best they could to get the gravely ill woman into the cockpit.

At least this time, when we watched the red cross lifting away, we felt it had regained some of its compassionate significance, and although we were never able to learn the ultimate fate of the poor American woman, we felt that she would soon be in good hands, in a Kathmandu hospital.

Mercifully Helen soon introduced a change of mood.

'That loo tent of ours is ridiculous,' she said crossly. This got our attention and we swung round to her and saw the tightly pursed lips. 'The bottom edge is two feet off the floor.' She paused. 'It doesn't leave much to the imagination, does it? – look at John in there right now. You can see halfway up his legs!'

'We burst out laughing, as only women and nurses can at the indignities of the bodily functions. We were still falling about when John emerged – not amused. He dismissed us with a few well-chosen words and stalked off to his tent.

Helen continued, 'You needn't think I'm going in there with it like that. From now on *I'm* going to take charge of the loo tent. *And* I'll get it right.'

'Will you be head of latrines then, Helen?' I said, still laughing. 'What are you going to do, dig the hole in the ground and pitch the tent yourself?'

'Don't be silly,' she replied grandly, 'I shall have my man do it, of course. Hari, I expect.' Her eyelids closed slowly and she sniffed, imperiously lifting her nose in to the air before she added, 'I shall just instruct.'

Mike Cheney (our trekking agent) had, with a gentlemanly concern for the ladies, provided a modest black loo tent which was usually erected by one of the cook-boys who, without any direction, or understanding of the reasons for such niceties, often sited it in an unsuitable position. Thus it often ended up on a slope or in a boggy patch or even indelicately near to our own tent. Helen, whose tolerance of this minor annoyance had obviously run out, decided to address the problem herself. OC Sadiq was about to go into action, and we therefore looked forward to the next camp, visualizing her striding about with Hari or Ang Panang walking dutifully three paces behind her, carrying the loo tent.

None of us girls had camped before, and we certainly weren't walkers, in the true hiking sense, like John and Terry, who had walked all over the place in the UK. We knew it was very brave of them to have taken us on in the first place and, the last two or three days aside, we'd had a great deal of fun, despite being faced with all sorts of practices new to us.

We learnt to wash with a flannel-full of water, as far down and as far up as you can go with your clothes on, and to conserve precious water by cleaning our teeth with our tea. At night we would fill our hot-water bottles with whatever was left over from the evening tea making and in the mornings we would lace it with purifiers and put it into our drinking bottles. Although this improvisation was all very foreign to us, we were rather surprised to find that we adapted to it quite well, and soon didn't mind it at all.

Probably the most often changed things were Helen's earrings. In her normal habitat, she enjoys glamorous clothes and she could see no reason why she should dispense with her glitzy earrings just because she was wearing thick-knee length khaki socks and heavy walking boots. These frivolities became another fairly accurate barometer of her mood. If she put the large, dangly ones on in the morning, then we knew she was feeling good, but if the discreet, simple studs went on then we knew she was tired – even before the day had started.

The following day, after a slow start, lots of rests and a drop in altitude, I felt the energy flowing back, and my legs felt strong again. We stopped for an early lunch, the sun rose high in the sky, giving us all new heart, and by the time we arrived, later that day, at Dingboche I was completely recovered.

We had three tents between us. The men had one each, and we women shared a larger one. Each evening we all had supper together in our bigger tent. John and Terry piled in, and Terry in particular regaled us with many funny stories, while Ang Panang, Mighty Atom (our nickname for him, because of a hat he wears marked Atom) and Hari cooked outside. Pemba and Mighty Atom would then bring the food to the tent.

We would guess a lot about the food. Would it be soup? Yes: we always had soup, a thin meaty broth, always hot and always welcome; dal, rice and/or boiled potatoes followed. Sometimes we'd get cabbage, tuna or omelettes and maybe chapattis. We usually guessed right about the first two courses, as they didn't alter, except for one night when Pemba produced yak steaks, which tasted like chicken. Once he had chased after a man carrying chickens up to Namche and tried to buy one from him. But the vendor wouldn't part with one: all or nothing he had stipulated. so we got nothing. I was glad, as they were still alive and squawking in the *doko*, and I didn't care to think about Pemba wringing their necks or cutting them with his *kukri*, an evil-looking Sherpa knife that is part of every mountain man's uniform. Sometimes the pudding changed, but only in colour. It might be brown mousse or pink mousse. To John, Terry and Susie it didn't matter – they loved them both – but Helen and I hated the mousse so we'd share a few Smarties – as long as I did the sharing. That meant that Helen got the brown, red and orange ones and I kept the apple-green, lilac and pink. Well, they were *my* Smarties!

Although Pemba and the boys slept rough and cold outside (sometimes in a tea lodge), he always brought us a battered old hurricane lamp at dinner to light and warm the tent. Each night, after dinner when he brought the *chi*, we would ask him about the next day. As usual, we asked him that night: 'What about tomorrow, Pemba, do you think we could get to Pangboche and see the monastery?'

Pemba spoke excellent English and Japanese, both learnt from the Japanese on his many climbing expeditions. Now he was hoping to be a top-class Sherpa guide, since the trekking phenomenon was growing rapidly. He thought it 'nice to show people his country' and 'good for money' but 'too much for mountain-village prices and some bad things happen, like stealing.' We expressed surprised at that, as the Nepalese are renowned as trusty, good, honest people.

'Not Nepalese,' he said, 'trekkers, they steal from each other. Yes, tomorrow I take you to Pangboche Monastery; no problem get in – if you make money to the monks – they show you head of yeti.'

'A head of a yeti?' we queried.

'Yes,' he insisted, nodding his head up and down, positively rejecting our doubts. 'Head of yeti – in Pangboche.'

'Is there really a yeti, Pemba – have you ever seen one?'

'No, but there is yeti,' he said adamantly.

We asked him to tell us about it. All this time Mighty Atom had been squatting, in the doorway of the tent, next to Pemba. The soft glow of the lamp lit their faces and cast dark, deep shadows behind them, and in this captivating chiaroscuro scene Mighty Atom's eyes never left Pemba's face. He listened, mesmerized, as Pemba related, with all the conviction of a true believer, the ancient lore of the yeti. He told of how it lived, part-man, part-animal, in the densely wooded hillsides or high up in the mountains. Of how its huge footprints had been seen many times, deeply imprinted in the high snows, and even low down near the villages. How it was feared, revered and venerated as a lesser god, and of how the skull of one was treasured in Pangboche Monastery.

We keenly anticipated seeing it, but we were now more fascinated by Mighty Atom. His rapt attention to Pemba's story-telling was particularly intriguing because we knew that he, a lovely, cheerful, round-faced boy, did not understand any English. Yet his attention had been fixed, as by a magnet, and as he sat, wide-eyed and enchanted like a child, he had in fact understood only one word: yeti. It was obvious that for him it was a mysterious, spine-chilling word, and it conjured up all the dark side of his folklore. It was a heady cocktail of something terrifying, something unknown, something magic and it held him fast in its spell.

4

The Birthday Party

A BUDDHIST monk beckoned us towards the tiny Pangboche Monastery. He ducked his shaven head under a low-beamed doorway, stepped over the threshold and led us into a walled courtyard. Its stone-flagged floor, slashed by strong sunlight and deep shadow, glowed with the patina of centuries of sandalled feet. The silent, serene, untroubled haven halted our chattering immediately. The tranquillity felt as if it was protected by the sheer strength and reassuring power of the massive timbers that framed the building and gracefully curved the roof up to the sky. We followed the monk, who shook his head at our cameras, and climbed the wide steps up to the great portal. The inner sanctum was a dark candle-lit chamber, and as the rhythmic hum of the OM MANI PADME HUM (O Jewel in the Lotus) mantra greeted us, we sensed the same reverence we had seen in Pemba's face last night.

The walls were almost completely covered in rich, formalized paintings, lovingly, painstakingly executed in the five mystic colours: red, blue, green, yellow and white. Stylized portrayals of Buddha, the blue Lord Shiva, Vishnu, Goddess Parvati slayer of demons, Ganashe the monkey god, and even tigers, elephants, birds, rats and serpents, were all brought into the service of religion, symbols of gods and demons, reincarnation and inner peace. The lotus blossom is used repeatedly. It symbolizes Buddha's pure soul and, as such, is central to the Buddhist religion.

Several monks, of all ages, sat beside the simple altar; they were lost in the repetitious chant of the mantra and a tinkling bell punctuated certain phrases. A mantra is used to protect the mind in transcendental meditation, as a device to shut out worldly distractions, impious thoughts and disruptive influences. It takes years of practice to implement properly, and we were about to witness a demonstration of it.

Slipping, as instructed, along the dark right-hand side of the room to a low bench, we sat for a while contemplating Buddhism, in all its simplicity, its purity, its striving for Nirvana through the spirit only and its rejection of excessive religious trappings. Then, through the gloom and incense, our attention was caught by an old crone wrapped in a ragged shawl sitting close to the monks. Every now and then she tinkled a bell which she picked out from a few simple possessions dotted about her. They included a chapatti lying at her feet on a crumpled piece of paper. At first she seemed mildly attentive to her bell ringing until an emaciated dog strolled in, stood for a moment in the shaft of sunlight at the door, and then started to sniff about the room. It snuffled over towards the chapatti, and when it showed more than a passing interest in the bread, she picked up a weapon and glared at it. The cur backed off, circling nervously, saliva dripping from its lolling tongue, weighing up its chances. She hissed warningly at it, but its courage came from hunger, and it dived at the chapatti. She raised the weapon and cracked it down, hard, on the dog's nose. It yelped in pain, and, as the weapon caught the light, we saw that it was a silver candle snuffer.

Helen, shocked by this casual use of an ecclesiastical treasure, leaned towards me and murmured out of the side of her mouth, 'Did you see that – she hit it with the candle snuffer!' Somehow she managed to give the act a terrible sense of naughtiness. I should never have looked at her, biting her lip to suppress the giggles, eyes alight with amusement and challenging me not to laugh, but I did, and it brought on a terrible fit. I stifled the sound with my hand, and darted an embarrassed glance at the monks – but the chanting flowed on. So did the battle – and, by now, the flea-ridden duo, apparently oblivious of the sanctity of this place, were locked in a full-scale tug of war. The air was filled with oaths and snarls . . . and the thrashing candle snuffer was flailing about only inches from the solemnly intoning monks – and still the chanting continued without missing a beat. But this dog-fight, in a place where one expects to find a tranquil kind of reverence, was just too much for Helen and me and, lacking the enviable control of the monks and shaking with silent laughter, not to mention feeling terribly guilty and embarrassed, we rushed outside. Seconds later the dog, complete with the spoils, streaked passed our legs and disappeared across the courtyard.

John wasn't far behind. He heaved a despairing sigh. 'I bring you all this way to experience the Buddhist religion and you collapse in hysterics at a dog, an old biddy, and a bit of bread.' But hearing him describe the scene only highlighted the incongruity of it all, and compounded our hysterics.

Another monk, smiling benignly behind John, apparently unperturbed by the silly, rude visitors, waved us towards a narrow staircase.

'He will show you the yeti head,' Pemba said, hushed with excitement.

'Come, come,' the old monk urged.

I wasn't sure if Helen and I were to be trusted with this piety thing, but John and Susie pushed us sternly towards the stairs, telling us to behave. At the top we were confronted by an open, carved, wooden screen, through which we saw a large room with wide, mellowed floorboards. The monk crossed over to a chest and pulled out a wooden box. He opened the lid and inside was a small skull, the yeti head. Lying beside it was a thin, dried, long-fingered hand covered with grey wrinkled skin. We craned to see it. Pemba peered over our shoulders. Our monk crooked his hoary hands under the precious relic and raised it up carefully. Pemba scanned our faces, waiting for our reaction, our appreciation.

It was a little hard to imagine that it really was a skull of a yeti – it seemed too small to match the size of the creatures in the stories and we could think of more likely animals to which it might have belonged – but in the final analysis all our scepticism seemed irrelevant. These people's beliefs and veneration were all that was important and so we joined them in their pleasure. After we'd made a small donation to the monastery, we sat for a while outside, listening to the transcendental chanting, drawing on its quiet strength.

Over the last few days Terry had grown quiet and unhappy, distancing himself from the group and complaining about the food, the walking and the cold. This behaviour was another manifestation of altitude sickness, and was indicative of strain and tiredness. Susie was concerned and we all felt for him, especially as the cold had caused painful sores on his mouth which were clearly making it difficult for him to eat and drink. That, combined with an unchanged diet for three weeks, hard physical effort every day and a growing feeling of homesickness, has a weakening effect and all contributes to dejection.

We knew how he felt, having grown physically tired ourselves, but overall the pleasures had outweighed the discomforts, and today we were not to be daunted because this was the day chosen for the birthday party. Pemba had asked over the last few days if we were going to drink the bottle of champagne and each time we told him, 'No, not this day, another day.' He laughed at the idea that a birthday could be movable, but when we told him that we had decided to save it until Namche Bazaar he was delighted, and with the customary hospitality of the Nepalese people he invited us to his home to celebrate it.

It was curious that he appreciated the concept of a birthday party, as generally the Nepalese don't recognize their own. They are not even sure of their own ages. Pemba thought he was about thirty-two and he was confident that his son was nine, but he didn't know his daughter's age, and he thought that his mother was about seventy, an unusually grand age in this country.

Before getting back to Namche Bazaar we had a visit to make, to Pemba's son's school at Kumjung. Travelling daily, uphill on rough mountain paths in all weathers, it takes him two hours to get there. It takes a little less time to get home, but often the latter half of the journey is in the dark. Nevertheless he attends from nine to three every day, except Sunday – and his school was considered near by Nepalese standards. This school was one of the many innovations, which include electricity, irrigation and piped water to the villages, initiated by Sir Edmund Hillary. His self-help programme for the Nepalese (now largely funded by New Zealand) began as a philanthropic gesture to reciprocate some of the pleasure he had himself received in Nepal, and it has now grown into a widespread improvement scheme.

Kumjung school, Hillary's first, is a fine example of the kind of work this great man, who is dearly loved in Nepal, has done. John, also with an unconscious commitment to community work, had made contact with our local school in Byfield and brought with him a collection of £32, and some letters from the children of Class 7 to the Nepalese children. He hoped they would make pen-pals. The headmaster introduced us to the twenty children of Kumjung's equivalent class. They sat in a sturdy classroom built with big chunks of stone by the villagers. The desks and benches were rough-hewn but functional and the walls were hung with maps, drawings and photographs. It was so cold in the classroom, however, that we couldn't imagine how these young children could concentrate. Obviously what was unbearable to us didn't appear to bother them (or perhaps their hunger to learn enables them to ignore such discomforts) and they listened attentively to John talking while the teacher interpreted. Later, John took photographs of the class to take back to the English school and we had a cup of tea with the headmaster. He explained that the teachers get a bonus to teach in these colder mountain schools, and that they have hostels for pupils who live several days' journey away. Later we went up to the hospital in Kunde (bigger than Periche's) to leave some of our drugs with them and visit the local artist.

When we arrived back we found that the boys had pitched our tent on one of the many tiered streets of Namche Bazaar – among the houses. Snow threatened. They indicated a (permanent) loo for us to use and Helen set off. She was back pretty sharpish.

'You needn't bother with that,' she announced as she crawled into the tent, interrupting us as we tried to spruce ourselves up (which only meant a wash and hair brush) for the birthday party.

'Why. What's wrong with it?'

'Wrong with it? I'll tell you: it's only got one side – it's a one-sided loo tent and it's open to the whole village!'

'You don't mean it!'

'Yes I do,' she said, 'and you'd better hope Pemba has something at his house, because it's just started to snow!'

'Oh, no. Oh well, never mind,' said Susie, who's always ready with some fortifying encouragement, 'I don't care. I just can't wait for the birthday party, and the shower tomorrow, the first in two weeks.'

'Oo, yes. What time did we book it for?' asked Helen, going into a reverie at the thought, snow already forgotten.

'Four o'clock tomorrow afternoon.'

'Do you think it will be hot?'

'Who knows,' I said. 'It depends on whether they get a good fire under it, I suppose, and then it might be like the loo – open to the whole village.'

'Oh no, don't say that,' said Susie. 'I'm not going to be put off – I'm sure it will be wonderful.'

One of Susie's most endearing strengths is her eternal optimism. Only three years ago she had developed lupus, a skin cancer, triggered off in her case by the sun. Being a nurse, she was alarmingly familiar with the prognosis of such a disease, and some of the finest doctors had left her with very little hope. They could only prescribe cortisone. But with her own immense powers of positive thought, unflinching determination, and by adopting a homoeopathic diet over two years, she'd fought the condition and cured herself. Tall, pale skinned, warm dark eyes and a crowning glory of thick, auburn curls, she charms everyone with her constant, sunny and caring disposition.

The electricity came on at dusk – four o'clock in Namche – the villagers being the proud owners of a generator. Pemba sent a couple of young lads to look after our tent, and we gathered up our personal belongings in our backpacks and set off with our torches to his house.

Pemba is not without importance in the village as he owns two houses, which he built himself with the help of his brother. He and his family live in one and his brother's family and mother live in the other, paying him a small rent. As an English- and Japanese-speaking Sherpa (shar means east, pa – people) guide, he earns money well above the average, which gives him a special status and deserved pride.

Most Nepali houses, of substantial wood and stone construction, are two-storeyed. The ground floor serves as a cattle manger and is noticeably warmed by the animals. When we stepped into Pemba's house, two huge yaks startled us by snorting in the dark as our torches caught their eyes. We hurried past, tripping on the feed sacks and *dokos* before we found the ladder at the back of the room. It led up to the main living area where Pemba was waiting for us.

This room was lit by two low-wattage bulbs. A log fire on a deep mound of ash burned under a square clay oven and water boiling in a pan wafted white steam into the smoky atmosphere. There was no chimney. Most of the smoke seeped out through the dense thatch, but a great deal never escaped at all and hovered thickly in the room, probably constituting the main cause of many of the people's chest problems. Highly polished, and proudly displayed on shelves, were copper and aluminium pots reflecting the vermeil glow of the fire. The shelves, covering two sides of the room, stretched from floor to ceiling. Blankets and boxes, some of which were marked with names of equipment manufacturers, were stacked neatly upon them. We turned to see Pemba's wife standing beside a rustic bed covered thickly in homespun rugs. Nestled in the folds of the covers was their youngest son, the one that Pemba's daughter had brought to meet him on that dreadful second day. He was their fifth child: two had died in childbirth.

Infant mortality is very high in Nepal. One of the main causes is bronchial due to the babies being carried on the mother's back while she leans over the smoky fire all day with the cooking. Their delicate lungs can't withstand the smoky onslaught and it weakens them considerably to the point that, should they suffer another illness, they have very little strength to survive it. When a mother goes into labour, the father moves out and the women (usually in-laws) move in. The babies are born, without modern aids or medicines, on just such a bed as this.

Mrs Norbu smiled graciously at us and held out her hand in welcome. There was no language barrier to our communication when she proudly showed us her hand-painted dishes and silver spoons on the dresser and we admired her necklaces made of amber, turquoise and silver beads. More beads were threaded into her waist-length plaits, and large wirework earrings cascaded down to her shoulders. The baby soon woke with the sound of our voices and after she had fed him he played, nappyless and unchecked, in the ashes of the fire. His head was swathed in smoke and he was too close to the flames for our comfort.

Mighty Atom, in a worn Fair Isle pullover, was squatting on his haunches beside the fire. He was surrounded by pans, plates and cooking utensils, his sleeves rolled up and his hands, probably unwashed, plunged up to the wrists in a bowl of dough. He grinned from ear to ear. We asked Pemba what he was doing.

'Cake,' he replied with pleasure. 'He makes the cake.'

'Cake?' we exclaimed, 'how lovely.' We were delighted with the unexpected treat.

Pemba beckoned us to a table at the other end of the room, where a curtain separated us from the cooking area. The celebrations began with a pitcher of *chhang*, a creamy-looking home-made beer brewed from distilled potato, and rather potent. Mrs Norbu poured it. Tradition calls for the glass to be topped up at least three times while you are drinking and Pemba's wife, diligent in her duties, stood back a little and watched for the slightest drop in the level of the beer in our glasses. It bore a remarkable similarity to methylated spirits, but we drank it gratefully. Luckily Mighty Atom was as diligent as Mrs Norbu and the food arrived in time to save us from a serious hangover the next day. He had specially made *keftas*, a small pocket of precious meat wrapped in rice-flour dough and deep-fried. We had potatoes (a staple crop of the mountain people), cabbage and rice, and, of course, Mighty Atom's cake. It was round, high and dusted with sugar. It looked good. We added a few Smarties, for a final touch, which pleased Mighty Atom and brought on one of his huge grins.

At last, we opened the champagne! Pemba was enjoying himself immensely, his dark eyes shining in the candle light, and when he saw the birthday card that Susie had given me, he asked if he could have it. It was a cartoon drawing of Margaret Thatcher and he wanted to put it up on his shelf alongside his photographs of the King and Queen of Nepal. It seemed to please him a great deal and he announced that he wanted to make a speech.

He spoke earnestly, saying that we had given him much pleasure. He hoped we had enjoyed his country and so forth and then he became rather solemn and philosophical, talking about his life and love of the mountains – telling us again how he hoped one day to be the best Sherpa in Nepal and climb one of the high mountains with an expedition. We asked him if there was anything that he would particularly like to have from England. Without hesitating he replied that he wanted a white stetson. This item, apparently, is *de rigueur* at one of Nepal's annual festivals, and when we said that we would send him one he was very excited.

All this, at what was beginning to feel like the end of our journey, was very moving and highlighted the empathy and bond that had grown up between Pemba and ourselves. There was more to come. He instructed his wife, who stood close by in the shadows but never joined us, to bring down a box from the top shelf. He opened it up and pulled out several *kattars*. A *kattar* is a white silk scarf that the Nepalese people like to present to special friends. It is an honour to receive one, and a symbol of their friendship and good wishes for luck and long life. He placed them, ceremoniously, around our necks and shook our hands. Mrs Norbu stood behind him smiling. I had a gift for him, too. A large dollar note in an envelope. A token of my appreciation of his efforts on my behalf. He didn't open it, nor did he thank me, but tucked it away without saying anything, and just smiled. It isn't their custom to open a gift in front of the giver or to say 'thank you'; their way is to return the gesture with another gift. I smiled also – it had been a most remarkable birthday.

When we woke the next morning we found the tent roc? had caved in under a heavy fall of snow and was only inches from our noses. However, it was market day in Namche Bazaar and, more important, shower day – we didn't care about the snow.

Peering out of the tent, we were amazed to see the market, not only gathering already, but no more than twenty or thirty yards away. People were milling all around our tent.

We passed the morning jostling among the crowds in happy market-day mood. Potatoes and onions were heaped up on pieces of cloth, and flour and rice spilled casually on to coils of rope and string. Boxes of matches and candles were stacked besides bolts of hand-printed material which in turn made comfortable nests for scrawny chickens. The egg lady shooed bleating goats away from her baskets of eggs and a trader with dozens of out-of-date films, in old biscuit boxes, tried hard to sell them to us as we took photographs. An old man cracked my camera with his stick in objection to me taking his picture. Some of the Nepalese, particularly the older ones, believe that the camera steals their spirit – that it leaves their body and goes into the image on the picture, and naturally they object to this. Generally we'd respected this feeling, and had always asked permission to take photographs as we travelled through the remote villages on the trail.

Soon the afternoon was on us and we three girls, filled with anticipatory pleasure, prepared the last of our clean clothes and headed off with a spring in our step to the shower. Unfortunately the shower owner wasn't prepared for three of us.

'Hot water for only one shower,' he announced. 'All take one – please – yes?' Seeing our disappointment, he continued, with an air of helplessness, 'The water is for one – it runs for a few minutes only.'

If we are lucky, we thought. 'Looks like we're all in together then.'

'Oh well, as long as we get a wash,' said Susie, 'that's all I'm worried about; we'd better make the most of it.'

Fortunately, when we got inside the shower-room we saw that there was enough space for three people to stand on the wooden duckboard together. Though we'd have to take it in turns to get under the pipe which jutted out of the wall. Helen started scrutinizing the earthy little hut.

'What are you looking for?' we asked. 'Cockroaches,' she said, 'or any other horrors,' which, in her case, meant spiders, and made me uneasy. I began to think about getting verrucas (shades of the fear of childhood visits to the public swimming baths rearing its ugly head, even after all these years!) and I decided that I wasn't going in there without socks on.

'For goodness' sake, Mags, after all you've put up with, you're afraid of verrucas!'

But the childhood conditioning was too strong and I thought I'd rather take the ribbing that was obviously coming my way than risk foot infection, so I pulled my thick walking socks back on. Crisp, cold air blew through the gaps of the planked wall, chilling us as we waited, huddled in tiny towels, for the water to flow. In time, it duly did and we laughed, wondering if it was being hand-pumped from the other side of the wall. At least it was hot, deliciously hot, and we revelled in it – swopping places under the slow flowing water, washing our hair and my socks. The sensation of finally feeling clean was 'magic', as John would have said, and we wondered if he and Terry had shared a shower.

Two more days down to Lukla, tired, tearful days. Susie, who had stoically born most of the strain of worrying about me, was over-drawn on her own strengths, and our walking days didn't get any shorter. The snowfall had made the route wet and muddy, and it was hard going. It was still very cold out of the sun and our overnight stay back at Phadking by the river cheered us up only a little when we discovered high stacks of sweet, newly-mown hay on the ground floor of the half-built lodge. We lay in it, nostalgically smelling its long-forgotten sweet smell, and soaking up its warmth for a while. Our evening meal was being cooked upstairs, but by the time it was ready the upstairs was so cold and draughty that we were glad to get back to our warmer sleeping bags with hot bottles.

We three girls talked endlessly in our tent, about the journey and our adventures. John always said that when he could hear us giggling he was happy, because he knew that we were all right, but during the last few nights we had grown quiet. Our tiredness, and Terry's low spirits, made us long for more comfortable places, and we realized that now, having been through what seemed to us the full emotional spectrum, we were ready to go home.

We walked into Lukla the following day anticipating the flight home tomorrow. We were scheduled to stay one night, then up and off in the small silver bird to Kathmandu. A comfortable night in the lodge with the proud sign of 'bar and cheminny' (*sic*) would be very pleasant, but it did feel quite strange to be in a room again. Ours had Scandinavian overtones, with pine boarding, bunks on all sides, and orange, black and aquamarine curtains. After supper (which I wish I hadn't seen the boys cooking, in a foul-smelling hovel) had came back to haunt us and sent us scuttling off into the darkness to find somewhere to deal with the problem, I was volunteered for the story reading – we did our share of Jeffrey Archer, but this sent the girls off to sleep while it kept me wide awake. Never mind; tomorrow we would decide which articles of clothing would be useful to Pemba, and the boys, and then back to Kathmandu and civilization, satisfied that at least some of us had got to Everest base camp.

Three days later we were still in Lukla!

The weather was not as King Birendra, the reigning monarch, had decreed: 'fine and sunny throughout the kingdom.' It was not bad, but not fine enough for a small plane to fly in these mountains, nor to land on the treacherous Lukla field. So we moved ourselves into the grand Lukla Lodge, which had about twenty bedrooms, one or two working loos and one hundred and fifty other stranded trekkers. Still that was two more loos than our Scandinavian room.

Each day was spent in the central reception area, first trying to obtain food, then establishing our chances of getting on a plane. John spent most of his time talking to other stranded trekkers trying to winkle out any information about passenger seat allocation, but that didn't yield much news. Meanwhile, Susie was quietly doing better negotiating our medical supplies (aspirin, plasters and harmless things) with the guy who owned the hotel, and seemed to have some sort of bargaining power with the pilots and locals. Pemba waited on the landing strip, with other guides, ready to sieze any opportunity should it arise. Helen and I whiled away the hours playing Scrabble with Terry and feeling the benefit of our humour, and Terry's stories, return with the warmth of the hotel and the amber glow of bottled beer.

One day two aeroplanes did come in. That created a comic scene. Two hundred trekkers, plus porters, hearing them coming up the valley, suddenly appeared from all kinds of boltholes in brilliantly coloured anoraks. It was a lottery as to who would be the chosen ones, and on fairly long odds at that, as there were only nineteen seats and two hundred people – and a lot of baggage.

A booked seat on a certain date played no part in the equation, and we learned that when push comes to shove pills have a lot of power – next to someone that Pemba knew. On the third day we found ourselves at the door of the plane, not guaranteed to get on it, but nearer to it. Pemba, who by now was looking like my clone in my sweater, boots and jacket, elbowed us through with authority, while the crew argued about the luggage. Pushing forward with other passengers made you feel like an evacuee in a war zone, and a big sigh of relief rippled through the cabin when finally the door closed behind us, and we were on. We looked back to see where Pemba was sitting. He wasn't on the plane. We were devastated, couldn't bear it, wanted to get off, hadn't said goodbye, couldn't go without him – and as the plane slowly trundled away, it dawned on us that he had characteristically forsaken his seat for our baggage.

The plane felt too heavy to take off. Slothfully, it rumbled down the terrifyingly steep strip. The engines revved violently, struggling to gain speed and lift us off. Surely we must take off soon, we thought, gripping our seats, not daring to speak or look out through the windscreen. The edge of the cliff rolled inexorably towards us, and we pushed back in our seats, eyes locked fearfully on to it, as we bumped violently over the rough field. Would it never lift? Up, up, up we willed it, and finally, painfully slowly, it left the ground, lurched over the edge of the cliff, swooped down sickeningly and gradually levelled out. Feeling sick, and silent with fear, we tried to remain calm, and prayed the plane would stay up. Maybe Pemba had missed the right plane, as there was no joy in the flight and the scenery received only a cursory glance of admiration. Eventually we saw Kathmandu and felt our prayers answered, but we felt cheated leaving Pemba like that.

We were pleased to see Mike Cheney, and told him about Pemba immediately.

'Oh, don't worry about him, he'll catch another flight, or run down.'

'Run down! How long will it take him to run down?'

'Three days', he said casually.

'But we leave in two!'

We were standing in the airport, checking baggage to leave Kathmandu for Karachi, not having come to terms with leaving Pemba without saying goodbye, knowing we'd touched each other's hearts, when we saw him, pushing his way through the crowd, still dressed in my shirt and sweater. We called out his name in excitement and pleasure, drawing him towards us, willing him nearer. People stopped and stared, stood back and let him through, and when he reached us we hugged and laughed and choked back the emotion. He'd brought us more gifts, which was a terrible, final, sad gesture and made the parting even harder. As we struggled through the last goodbyes he placed his hands together again gently, looked tenderly at us with his warm eyes, and with the deepest feeling, softly murmured, 'Namaste.' We all smiled bravely.

PART TWO

1

K2. Anglo-American Expedition

I N the following January we received a letter from John, which read, 'What about trekking to K2, with an Anglo/American expedition? In May–June.' We were a little surprised at the idea and I remember standing with the letter in my hand and thinking – K2!

We had quite made up our minds to go trekking in the Himalayas again because, by now, we thought we knew all the pitfalls and we were hooked on the adventure; but we were thinking about something soft, something gentle and relaxing, like following rhododendron trails, idling through mountain villages and taking time to absorb the atmosphere, the culture and the scenery.

K2, on the other hand, being the second highest mountain in the world, and situated in one of the coldest, most remote places of the world, didn't seem to fit our bill, so naturally John's suggestion came as a bit of a shock.

Climbers call it 'the savage mountain'; with good reason, as it's claimed many lives – thirteen in the summer of 1986 alone – and it is universally acknowledged as the most difficult mountain to climb. Those same tough, intrepid types also say it's the hardest 'walk-in' there is to any mountain. Pete Boardman said, 'Next to climbing the mountain it is the most difficult thing I've ever done.' The route to it goes over desert areas, glaciers and big rivers and it is ten days from the nearest village. It wasn't the sort of undertaking we had had in mind. However, since John had planted the idea we, although still very dubious, had to admit that we were a bit intrigued.

John leant against my kitchen sink; he gave us the background: 'The expedition is being led by Doug Scott and they want to take a group of fifteen trekkers, to help defray the costs. It's the chance of a lifetime to go to K2 as, for years, only expeditions have been allowed to go there because of the Indian/Pakistani troubles. Now they've given permission for trekkers to go with the expeditions.'

We didn't even know where it was and I asked teasingly if it was in India. 'No,' he said, 'it's on the Pakistan-China border.'

'Near Everest?' Susie asked.

'No.' I couldn't help smirking as he winced. 'In the Karakoram.'

'Where's that then – in the central Himalayas?'

'No, in the western end of the main Himalayan chain – about eight hundred miles north-west of Everest, in northern Pakistan. Bit cold there though, I think,' he said carefully, knowing that we wouldn't like that. 'That's why K2 is so difficult to climb: because they get terrible blizzards on the mountain and the conditions are inclined to be even more treacherous than most. There's six climbers going; Doug and his son Mike, Greg Childs, Steve Svenson.' He counted on his fingers and furrowed his brow. 'Tim McCartney-Snape, an Australian, Phil Ershler from Seattle, who's a doctor I think. Oh, and, er, Doug's suggesting that if the conditions are suitable and there's enough time he will try to take those who'd like to up to Windy Gap, that's about twenty-one thousand feet.' He rubbed his hands and smiled with pleasure at the thought of this. 'What do you reckon?'

'Is it pretty?'

'What, Windy Gap?'

'No – pretty like Nepal. Will we see the rhododendrons, in May?'

'No. It's not quite like that; I don't think so anyway.' He grinned sheepishly and we began to worry. 'Anyway, you should see Concordia. That's where the Baltoro Glacier and the Godwin Austin Glacier converge and are surrounded by several eight-thousand metre peaks; Throne Room of the Gods they call it.'

'Just a minute, John, umm, now correct me if I'm wrong,' I said jokingly, 'but so far you've said it's cold, it's remote, it's hard walking, it's not very pretty, it's a long way, and you want us to go with a group of men we don't even know.' I paused for effect. 'Is there anything we would like about it do you think?' We all grinned at this and awaited his reply with bated breath.

'Well,' he said, dragging the word out slowly, but thinking fast, 'what about the fact that not many women have been up there? Probably only a handful – apart from women climbers, I mean. I don't know for sure, but it can't be very many, it's been such a closed shop. You could be in the first one hundred Western women to have trekked to K2,' he said smiling at us quizzically. He waited – to see if he'd sprung the trap.

The silence was heavy. We looked at each other, screwed up our

faces, read each other's thoughts and sensed that we were all nervously tempted. Then Susie confirmed, 'If one goes we all go, right?'

'Oh Lord,' Helen said.

John beamed.

'Looks like that's it then,' I said. 'From the kitchen sink to K2.
Right?'

As it turned out only Susie, John and I arrived in Pakistan the next
June. Helen had stayed behind. Earlier in the year, she and I had
walked from Belfast to Dublin on a charity walk for leukaemia
with Ian Botham and she had pulled a tendon in her right knee.
Unfortunately the injury was quite severe and made this kind of
arduous walking completely out of the question for her. Of course,
we were all terribly disappointed, and Susie and I knew we were
going to miss her.

Now, we three had joined the rest of the group of K2 trekkers
and arrived at Rawalpindi airport about noon. Heat, humidity and
humanity enveloped us as we waited for the bags. It was a little
cooler outside, but the pavements were just as crowded, and entire
families seemed to be living on them. Some were even asleep and a
soft rain fell on them.

Two buses were waiting to take us to the hotel. They were painted
vividly, fringed in chainmail and sported religious talismans on their
radiators. The jolly, chrome exterior disguised the rather dilapidated
interior, where the seat-covers had faded in the hot sunshine and
the springing was long gone, but there was something friendly and
comfortable about them – like an old sofa.

The rain was too fine to douse the heat, or lay the dust and it
swirled all around us as we rattled along the pot-holed roads to
Islamabad. A few, fume choked marigolds bloomed bravely in a thin
spine of flowerbeds down the centre of the road, but the jacaranda
trees, which lined it, were faring better and a haze of dusty blue
flowers arched over the scene.

Our driver reeled the bus from side to side, negotiating the hazards
of the busy road which buzzed with life, while we stared out of
the window at the frenzied activity. Here, motor scooters provided
transport for four people; father drove, mother sat side-saddle in
her sari holding the baby, and another child, standing on the
opposite pedal, clung to her back. Bleating herds of goats, being
driven along the gutter, darted erratically into the road and caused

the immediate traffic to swerve wildly. Waves of cyclists would swell out, pedalling furiously, around more prosperous passengers in trishaws, which were being pulled by lean, emaciated men. Rumbling camel-carts, overloaded with twenty-foot-long steel rods, travelled at what seemed to be unstoppable speeds. Everyone went about their business, and even those on foot were loaded with goods which were piled either up on their heads, or carried in panniers at their sides.

Only the omnipotent water buffaloes, ironically themselves causing some of the chaos, seemed calm. They lay randomly in the road, eyes blinking serenely, but as the reincarnation of the sacred mother, they are protected from harm by Islam.

By now we had met the only other woman who had joined the trek, Polly Quick, who came from Stratford and was much younger than Susie and me. After the long journey, she, like us, had been looking forward to getting to the hotel; it sounded so romantic — the Scheherazade.

We should have guessed better. It had none of the Eastern promise, or sultry, exotic charm suggested by its romantic name. In fact it was an ugly building, made of concrete and dotted with dying plants. Even the plastic plants hanging from the balconies had an air of despair about them. We trod the worn, torn carpet carefully, Susie, Polly, and me, dragging our bags behind the non-bag-carrying porter until we were delivered into a large, dingy bedroom. The porter indicated the en-suite bathroom and pointed out the shower proudly. We looked at the rusty pipe glumly. The only thing likely to come out of there, we thought, would be crawling on eight legs. We studied the bucket of water standing on the slimy floor and speculated as to its purpose: washing? Flushing the loo? Its secret was secure. Four metal-framed beds and a rickety table furnished the room and tattered, pewter-grey curtains that Miss Haversham would have been proud of blocked out the sun. Susie banged the window with the heel of her fist. It burst open but only let in the roar of the street. I sat on the bed, feeling disenchanted, and watched the girls start to unpack.

John walked into the room. 'Come on, girls, lunch in the greasy spoon café. Aren't you starving?'

'Oh, yes. What do you think it will be? A salad would be nice in this heat,' Susie said.

It was a curry, or at least curried sauce covering something hard to define. The rice was oily, the forks unpleasant, the drinking water cloudy, and the glasses were covered in something equally hard to define.

Immediately after this culinary shock John and I went in search of loo paper, which the hotel didn't keep, and some bottled water. We probed a few shops, which all seemed to be strangly devoid of people. Sand lay in drifts against old tin boxes stacked on the floor among an eclectic array of anachronistic items like Pear's soap, Capstan cigarettes, Fry's cocoa, Vimto and reels of cotton still on wooden bobbins lay forgotten on dusty shelves. We felt we'd stepped back fifty years into a period set of a British corner shop during the war. It was as if the Brits had never left, and now these shops were an Alladin's cave of collectable memorabilia. Delightful though this nostalgic stroll was, we though we'd better pursue the loo rolls and in doing so came across hessian sacks of gloriously-coloured aromatic spices, heaped up in cone shapes and giving off the most pungent and exotic smells. Ah, India, I thought – getting closer.

John, Polly and Brian Lee, one of the trekking party, decided to go into Rawalpindi, leaving Susie and me at the hotel, lying on our beds. Susie soon fell asleep and I wondered, as I heard her book slip from her fingers, whether Morpheus had carried her back to England, to her husband and her two daughters, and if she was dreaming of happy times in Dorset. The curtains moved listlessly in the heat, and as I cast about the room my eyes fell on the huge air-conditioning unit barnacled to the wall above my bed. I looked at it longingly, but sadly it looked as if it had been lifeless since it was installed, unlike the scary electrical wiring, which was nailed across the ceiling in loops, with its switches hanging heavily off the end of the wire. They promised an even bigger shock than the hotel had already given us, so we'd decided to do without the lights.

The contents of Polly's kitbag were strewn over her bed, discarded until her return from Pindi. Who was Polly? How would we fare together, we three? Polly, a pretty, petite girl with lovely olive skin and dark glossy hair, was a keen climber, and had come to K2 alone. She was now assigned to live intimately with Susie and me for a month, since 'the three girls together in the three-man tent' had been the unilateral decision by the trek organizers. Now that we were without Helen they had presumed that Polly would fit in with her new companions, assuming that we would be compatible. But whether our personalities would run smoothly together, like rushes in the shallows, remained to be seen. We hoped so, as a small tent, shared in difficult conditions, needs harmony, but Polly laughed and talked easily and we couldn't help but like her.

Susie and I had been intrigued to see what she had brought with her. 'Has she got things that we might not have thought of?' we asked. 'Has she brought make-up, a mirror, perfume?' We needed her reassurance about these things as they seemed like fripperies to take to K2. She had – also a couple of books to swop, medicines and crampons.

'CRAMPONS! *Why?*'

'To go to Windy Gap,' she replied. We were impressed. We only hoped to get to base camp, as the altitude problems were still fresh in our minds, and we were fearful that not only would Windy Gap be synonymous with its name, but, more to the point, far beyond our capabilities.

On our way to dinner we found Doug and Mike ankle-deep in climbing equipment, spread all over the landing. Other climbers were sitting against the wall. They looked tired. The flights had been long and it was stiflingly hot. Doug was trying on warm climbing suits. He was sweating in the heat and probably in some pain, as he had four broken ribs, from a riding accident. He was hoping they would heal before the climb! The group were deciding which equipment to take, and trying to pare it down to the absolute essentials, as carrying gear is always a problem.

We gathered on the pavement outside and hailed the yellow and black Morris Minor taxi cabs, and when we'd squeezed four or five people into each the Pakistani drivers began their death-defying deliverance of innocents abroad. With one arm resting on the open window, one hand poised over the horn as a kind of radar through clouds of dust and bicycles, they drove crazily through the streets to the Golden Dragon 'Chinese' restaurant. The required bargaining over the taxi fare was settled and we went inside. There was no electricity and the room was lit by candles. The waiter assured us that we could have hot food, but that it would take some time. Imagining the meal to be cooked over slow candle power, we left. However, on we went to another 'Chinese' restaurant, with a very friendly *maître d'*, and I made my first acquaintance with Greg Childs, who was sitting beside me and whispered that he had a few thousand dollars, expedition expenses, in his knapsack – and would I keep an eye on it! Steve Svenson, sitting opposite, exhausted after the long flight from Seattle, folded his arms on the table, lowered his head and slept throughout the entire meal. Susie talked to Carolyn, the only female member of the climbing party, and discovered that, although she was really a veterinary surgeon from Denver, she had come along as the doctor-cum-cook for the climbers.

It was still dark in the morning when we staggered out of the hotel with our bags. The lads loaded them on to the roof of the minibus. A brilliant crescent moon in a black sky reminded us how early it was. A tarpaulin was thrown over the lumpy pile and lashed down with an old fraying rope. Little did we realize then what an integral part of our lives these 'tarps' would become. A smiling man from the hotel brought us thick black coffee and we drank it as we watched the geckos running about the courtyard. They were funny little things, all urgent and anxious, able to stop dead in a split second, freeze, heads up, look, listen and then on again like a flash of quicksilver.

All aboard the bus for Skardu in Baltistan, with Susie and me on the back seat. It was five hundred miles and we expected it to be a bit rough. We rattled and bumped our way out of Islamabad and, picking up the Karakoram Highway, travelled north-east following the Indus river through Kashmir towards Gilgit. We made one over-night stop and before Gilgit turned east to Skardu, which lies a hundred and fifty miles from the China border. Had the weather permitted we would have taken the flight through mountain scenery reputedly the most spectacular in the world, up the Hunza valley past the mighty peaks of Nanga Parbat (26,650 ft) and Rakaposhi (25,545 ft) to Skardu. As the weather did not permit it, however, we hoped that we would be able to fly back, and settled down to seeing the famous Karakoram Highway.

Twelve happy trekkers had got on the bus at Rawalpindi: Susie, John, Polly, Brian Lee (a nurseryman from Leicester), Brian McMahon (an arboriculturist), Edwin Wallage (an engineer), young Mark Fox (who worked for British Telecom), an older man called Paul Spriggs, Alistair Bridge (a builder), the quietly-spoken Keith Gardener, Malcolm Otter (a chemist, and our co-trek leader) and me. Doug and the rest of the climbers were hoping to get away tomorrow when the two Americans, who were filming the climb, arrived.

Twelve stiffened, bruised trekkers were never so glad to get off the bus, two long days later. The Karakoram Highway (or the KKH, as it's known) had stamped a lasting impression on both our minds and our battered bodies. It is cut through the highest, most unstable mountains in the world and follows the ancient Silk Route, said to be taken by Marco Polo, which crosses northern Pakistan, the

Khunjerab Pass at 15,416 ft, China's high plateau, skirts the edge of the Gobi Desert and ends in Beijing. In all the road is nearly 3,400 miles long, a route travelled by traders and their animals from east to west since time began. It's an extraordinary construction cut out of solid rock along the gorges and is often barely wide enough for two vehicles to pass. It took twenty years to build, 15,000 men and cost many lives. But the vastness of the mountains dwarf the road to such a degree that it appears as slender as a tendril of vine. The young mountains move frequently and the road snaps as easily as a filament of sugar, requiring an army of maintenance men to keep it open. One landslide after another slips muddily across the road and the repair teams often have to work with boulders pinging down on them from above. Lorry drivers are said to drive with their doors open to allow them to jump clear quickly should they encounter these hazards.

We twisted and wriggled, wriggled and twisted, and bumped up every one of those five hundred miles to Skardu. Much of the time we were a thousand feet above the river, on a sliver of road, being driven by a tired driver in impossible heat. Although a nervous tension about the road pervaded much of the journey, the stark, solid grandeur of the gorges containing the raging Indus held much of our attention.

When we eventually passed Skardu airfield, at 7,498 feet, and looked wistfully at it, we saw that it was shrouded in a vast cloud of sand. It would have been impossible to land there.

Skardu's wide main street was a teeming mass of men and boys dressed in the ubiquitous *shalwar-kameze* (cotton suit). There were no women to be seen. It led to the bungalow-style K2 Hotel, on the banks of the upper Indus. The support trek leader, Steve Razzetti, was there waiting for us. It seemed there was a problem: a Norwegian expedition had arrived two days previously and fully occupied the hotel, and they were not ready to vacate. The proprietor, who had two rooms left, containing six beds, suggested that the rest of us pitch our tents in the garden outside and use the bathrooms inside. We were learning to take life as it came, and the outside was, in any case, cooler, so we made our first camp in the garden of the K2 Hotel, Skardu.

Because of the heat, which we now understood could be as much as 107 degrees on the glaciers, Malcolm thought it would be wise for each of us to buy ourselves a *shalwar-kameze* to wear on the trek. We decided to do this later in the day. After hiring a car and a six-fingered driver (not uncommon in these parts) with the tinniest Asian taped music in the world to take us to the highest reservoir in the world (Satpara Lake), we made our way back to the bazaar in Skardu.

Our presence in the narrow streets aroused enough interest to bring out an English-speaking Baltistani, who led us to the tailor's little cabin. Three men sat in the lotus position, elbow to elbow, at sewing machines. The 'tealir-master', as he called himself, proffered cushions, plied us with sweet tea, and bowed a lot while wringing his hands like Shylock. Boys rolled out bolts of cloth in the dusty road for our approval and while we made our selection local men and children, pressing from all sides, scrutinized every detail of us. When the tailor took out his tape and measured the sahib's inside leg, and the memsahibs' busts, they giggled openly, obviously enjoying the joke. It was nice to see that their strict Muslim religion didn't dampen a natural sense of humour. The cloth and measurements were recorded and when we asked for three extra suits, seven in all, by tomorrow, he smiled beatifically, shook the men's hands warmly and said, 'All seven suits will be ready by tomorrow afternoon, sir – do not worry, please, thank you.' He bowed us away, intoning, 'Sh'alla malla cum.' We tried to get our tongues around this traditional salutation (which, broadly speaking, means, like the Nepalese, God go with you), thanked him very much and left.

The climbers had arrived and they spent the day making final preparations at the expedition's depot. The film crew – Allen Blaisdale (director), Steve Marts (the renowned climber/photographer) and Shadid Zaidi (a cinematographer) – arrived with Shadmeena from Islamabad. Shadmeena was to be the film crew's liaison officer and was the first female in Pakistan ever to rise to that rank, something of an achievement in such a male-dominated society.

The following day, in extreme heat, we took a trip to Shangri-La. Suffice it to say we had a blissful afternoon there, just as one would expect in a place named after the mythical paradise. The tiny holiday resort is a favourite wateringhole of Pakistanis on the grand tour through the hill countries of Kashmir and the Hunza. For a few rupees a colourful rowing boat can be hired, complete with striped awning, and one can bob about on the crystal lake after a lunch of trout in the pagoda-style restaurant.

We came back, past Skardu's fort, through a lashing dust storm driven by a fierce wind that slides down the mountains most afternoons. It whips up the sand from the river bed and curls it around in mini-tornadoes. It buffeted and blasted the jeep as we drove along. We soon found ourselves pulling our scarves over our heads and across our faces, imitating Arab dress and appreciating why they wore their big scarves.

That night Malcolm played his harmonica, sang songs and recited a lengthy poem called 'Three Ha'pence a Foot' in pure Stanley Holloway. Frogs were put into girls' sleeping bags and a lot of terrible jokes were told. We were beginning to get to know one another, beginning to cohere as a group, and getting very excited about setting off tomorrow.

2

Shigar. Valley of Adam

A<small>T</small> 7.30 a.m. the jeeps were packed with our bags at the hotel ready to take us up to the road-head. It was already hot. Five of us scrambled up into a jeep and settled down among the baggage in the least lumpy spot. Our legs, umbrellas and walking sticks, intimately intertwined, locked us all together. Two in the cab and Malcolm riding 'shotgun' seemed like a case of overload, but we looked on it as part of the adventure and our convoy snaked through the streets of Skardu to the depot. Here we loaded more equipment and when we were within a hair of breaking the vehicle's back, by adding more bulging blue barrels in which the expedition equipment was packed, the Doug Scott Anglo-American Expedition set off for K2.

To cross the upper Indus we rumbled over Skardu's new articulated bridge, which rolled in waves under our weight. We then turned north-east across the desert plains, which shrouded the jeeps in sand, towards the mountain villages of Shigar and Dassu. From there we would start the walk-in.

Within an hour we were stopped. The road was being peppered by prodigious boulders bouncing down the mountainside. Somewhere higher up they were blasting a new road (part of a tourist programme) and after much deliberation among the leaders we were hailed on and our driver crawled along the outside edge of the road, perilously near its steep drop, while we scanned the air for flying boulders.

I dwelled, unhappily, on the prospect of new roads. Did this mean that the floodgates would soon be open to these few remaining unspoilt corners of the world? Would this remote region soon be accessible to mass tourism 'easy style'? It was a worrying thought and I wondered if these small communities couldn't be adequately serviced on the same rough tracks, but with superior vehicles. The villages would then seem less attractive to commercialism and to developers with no desire to conserve. Perhaps this was a selfish view; after all, I didn't have to live in this region with its many inconveniences, and maybe it is the valley people themselves who want the road, but as far as visitors, foreigners, trippers were concerned, surely we could go elsewhere for comfort and thus leave these remote mountains for real grass-roots orienteering? But man is frighteningly tenacious when it comes to spoiling the environment for commercialization, and although we have ski lifts at the ski slopes, golf carts at the golf course and motor boats even on the tiniest lakes, it's still never quite enough. The important question, of course, is: will the Baltistanis actually be the true beneficiaries of the indiscriminate siting of hamburger joints and the like in their mountains?

The utilitarian vehicles were incredibly uncomfortable, but they couldn't diminish the pleasure of driving through the Shigar valley. It was one of the most beautiful, exciting and happy experiences I have ever had. The valley is a scene at once of sensational drama and blissful calm. A fortress of towering mountains, set against the blue sky, guards the sunlit valley from the world, while the crisp clean air, vibrant with bird-song, has a sense of sparkling energy about it from the young Indus.

The village of Shigar is canopied by willows, apricot trees and slender spines of bamboo. We approached it through fields of wheat and barley, all shimmering and velvety and stippled with wild flowers. When Kipling said, 'Adam was a gardener' I'm sure he was inspired by just such a valley as this.

Further on, at Dassu, two hundred local men waited for the expedition and we learned that not only was Doug Scott a familiar, loved figure but that they pronounced his name 'Duss-cart'. One hundred and fifty of them would be selected as porters, but not in Dassu; for that they had to go on to the camp site at Brianso, two hours' walk away. The quicker, sharper ones hooked themselves on to the backs of the jeeps and hitched a ride.

At the camp site, the thin air was immediately noticeable when we hauled the kitbags across the grass to a bushy ledge, above the main camp.

Malcolm climbed up behind us. 'You're going to camp up here, are you?' he asked us three girls.

'Yes, is that all right?'

'Fine, I'll get your tents,' he said and skipped back down the slope; but he was puffing hard when he returned with a blue barrel containing our tent, and with obvious relief he dumped it at our feet. 'See what you can do with that,' he said, nodding and winking at the other men – and leaving.

Now that would seem an innocent enough remark to anyone else, but it stopped us dead in our tracks: Susie and I had never put up a tent before.

'Well that's a joke,' I said, not quite believing he meant us. We looked around.

'Don't look at me, girls,' John said. 'I haven't put one up either; I've always had a Pemba.'

'Polly, you must have done this. You know how to do it, don't you?'

'No, I don't,' she said hurriedly with a grin, 'not one like this anyway.'

'Listen, just make a start,' John said with an impatient flap of the hand. 'If you can't manage it, we'll come and help in a minute.' He strolled off to look at his own tent.

'Pemba, where are you now?' Susie joked.

'Anybody got any ideas?' I asked, holding up a bundle of gilt-coloured poles. They were folded!

'Folded poles; what are we supposed to do with these?' the girls wailed and we heard a heavy sigh drift over from the men.

And so it was in the beginning; we puzzled over our jigsaw of a tent. 'This folded pole goes through that slot – no, that pole goes through there – I think – or perhaps it goes in here – is it the same as that one – no, this has got a curve on it – well, perhaps it goes in there then – or even in here – no – that's right – that's wrong.' This was our conversation for some time. Meanwhile the khaki canvas lay sprawled across the grass, formless, unco-operative and thoroughly irritating. We waited for the one per cent inspiration (ninety-nine per cent perspiration we had), the mystery to unfold, something – help even – and eventually it came in the form of Brian and Ed.

And so we erected the cosy little house which would be home for the next twenty-two days. Some would say it was *too* cosy for three people, and that's just what Doug *did* say when he saw it, or words to that effect.

'Not much bigger than a dog kennel, really, is it?' he said humorously, so Polly volunteered to sleep outside – on the warm nights!

We had a splendid view of the camp and I watched the jazzy chemical colours of the Western group moving about, contrasting sharply with the natural, earthy tones of the porters flooding into the camp. Many of them made straight for the shade of the two walnut trees. Greg strode by, loaded with a thirty-pound pack. He was about to tackle the 300-foot cliff behind us, to keep fit. Suddenly there was a commotion among the porters.

'It's a porters' meeting,' Tim told us, and we wandered over to watch. Allen and Steve rushed by to set up their tripods. Soon, with their faces buried in the lens, they were shouting and waving frantically at all extraneous, drifting people to get clear of the frame.

Approximately two hundred porters squatted on their haunches at their leader's feet. Their eyes, like those of worried schoolchildren, never left his face. He stood a little way up the bank, like God on the mount directing his disciples, in Urdu. The cameras rolled. He was autocratic, powerful and stout, and the porters were nervously respectful of him. He was about to select the one hundred and fifty porters that we needed. Not all of them would get a job. The chosen ones were called out from a list and sent to sit in rows, one behind the other. An over-zealous senior porter continually straightened up the rows by prodding the men with a stick and nodding at them to keep the line straight. Obediently, they shuffled tightly in behind each other. Every porter was given a disc with his number on it. This related to his allotted load, between forty and fifty pounds; the stronger ones would carry more, and be paid accordingly.

Eventually we had three rows of men: the climbers' porters (ninety of them); the film crew's porters (thirty); the trekkers' porters (thirty) and finally porters' porters. Each group was headed by a *sirdar*. Ours (the support trekkers') is called Nabi. It took a great deal of time to organize all this. The leader, still standing six feet above contradiction, dominated the proceedings throughout. At one point a slight, brave man argued with him and received a few blows about the head for his trouble, but even as the porter stared coldly back, it was clear that he had just lost his load.

I went to the tent to write my diary; the others went to a waterfall to wash. I hadn't been writing long when Malcolm climbed up our little slope and threw himself down on the grass. He let out a great sigh.

'What's the matter then, Malc?'

'Oh nothing,' he drawled, 'I'm just having a crisis.'

'What is it, then?'

'Nothing really,' he repeated with an even bigger sigh. 'It's just organizing everything, making sure everyone has got what they need

– and – oh, I don't know really.' He picked at the grass. 'I think I'm just a bit tired; it's been a long hot day, hasn't it?' and he rolled over on to his back and chewed on the sliver of grass in his hand.

'Yes, it really has – bit of a military operation getting an expedition of twenty-five-plus and a hundred and fifty porters away without any hitches, isn't it? Although I'm sure that the climbers look after themselves, don't they?'

'Yes, of course they do; we're quite separate really in that respect. It's our group, the trekkers, which we, as the trekking agency, are responsible for, all your kit and food. That's what I'm trying to get settled.'

'Oh, don't worry, it'll be all right. Anyway, we can't change things now, can we?'

'No, not really; still, I think I'll just stay up here for a while, out of the way. Till I've cooled off,' he said, hinting at some altercation.

'You think you've got troubles – what about me? I don't know how I'm going to get across that bridge tomorrow. I'm terrified of them, you know.'

He sat up on one elbow. 'Seriously?' he exclaimed. 'What happened in Nepal then, when you went to Everest?' He sounded rather surprised.

'That was the problem. That's where I discovered I didn't like swinging Tarzan-type rope bridges. It's feeling it swing and seeing the swirling water through the rope struts and not having much to hang on to that I can't stomach. It makes my head reel and I freeze. I know they're strong enough, I suppose, because the yaks go over them – even if the porters do have to whack 'em to get them over, but, now, the prospect of having to get in a "bucket" and being swung over the Braldu Gorge terrifies me!'

'Oh, don't worry about it; we'll get you over,' he said with deliberate nonchalance – 'somehow.' He grinned at me.

'I hope so!' I said, and we avoided the subject from then on and laughed at the sardine stain on the front of his new white *shalwar-kameze*.

It was only the first day and, already Malcolm looked hot, bothered and scruffy like a little urchin, a naughty boy in need of a good wash and a big cuddle. He seemed to pull at the heart-strings and evoke all our mothering instincts. It was these boyish qualities that would charm us all in the end, including the porters. It brought out the nurse in Susie and made her long to dunk him in a stream and

scrub him from top to toe. She did, eventually, make him wash, but
it was five days later.

With the sun setting and business over, the porters, in groups of
five or six, lit small fires to cook their chapattis and brew *chi*. After
Malcolm had gone I sat and watched them, wrapped in their yak-
wool blankets and hunched over their fires. A sea of flat, *chitral*
hats, themselves looking like chapattis, nodded in conversation. The
warm browns and slate greys of their clothes, their black hair and
swarthy skin made them hard to distinguish from the rocky outcrops.
In the dusk, without movement, or the murmur of their conversation,
or the bright dots of crimson from their cigarettes, they would have
been invisible. An animal would smell 'man,' but man, who relies
on vision, would be fooled. It was camouflage in its purest, original
form. How many centuries back was I looking, I wondered? Man,
land, fire, water – the very warp and weft of life – all inextricably
entwined. How soon would all this harmony be swept away when
the great wave of commercialism flowed in on the new road called
Progress, I wondered?

A cook beat a tattoo on a saucepan. 'Grub up!' someone called,
and my mellow thread of contemplation was broken. A patterned
plastic tablecloth laid on the grass created the dining scene and we
sat on small folding stools around it in the warm evening. We ate
pasta, peas and ham in a sauce, and a sort of semolina with jam or
chocolate mousse.

Doug mentioned the bridge, attempting to reassure those who
might be nervous. 'It's easy,' he said, and he went on to talk about
the possibility of not getting to Windy Gap. This was a very important point for the would-be mountaineers among the trekkers, as it
was a goal they would very much have liked to score. But we all
knew that fatigue, time, and especially weather tend to shift the
goalposts and that we would therefore have to be flexible.

The group was finally complete: twenty-five in all, climbers, film
crew and trekkers. Then there were the liaison officers (conscious
of their station, especially with the porters), the *sirdars*, the cook-
boys and the porters.

Long after supper, just as we were looking for a soft patch of
grass to sleep out on, we heard the porters singing, and looking
across the camp saw them gathered around a big fire. It wasn't long
before we answered their siren call and hurried across, through the
darkness, towards the fire. Their eyes were lit by the fire's glow and
the drumming quickened as people came from all sides. To our

amazement we saw Razzu (the cook) whirling about like a dervish in a trance. His face was horribly distorted and manic, as he spun wildly around in the eerie light. Two small sticks were wedged between his nostrils and bottom lip. They curled his mouth back so that he resembled a snarling wolf. Nabi whipped up the clapping and the drumming grew faster and louder. Razzu, more and more wild-eyed, darted at the audience displaying his fangs and he laughed demonically at us, as we recoiled. The fever pitch and swirling made him stagger dangerously near the fire, his bare feet missing the white-hot embers by inches. Suddenly he dropped like a stone and lay in an ecstatic trance. For a moment we felt nervous for him, thinking he had passed out, but then we realized that he was revelling in the applause and enjoying every minute of his audience's appreciation. The film crew captured it all.

With Razzu's performance over, Nabi set about trying to persuade us, particularly the women, to join in and dance in the circle. He persuaded Malcolm easily, and Susie with more difficulty. I disappeared like greased lightning behind a few of the men, only to find Polly already hiding there! Poor Sue was thus left on her own.

After it was over she told Nabi she'd enjoyed it, but saved a few more choice words for Polly and me for not supporting her. Malcolm had loved it, of course. His unabashed, genial temperament had found a natural outlet, much to the delight of the porters.

Eventually we drifted back to our grassy bank. Weary and ready for bed, we slipped into our sleeping bags and watched the stars in the light-streaked sky. Up here, the Great Bear, which I always think of as an old friend and look for every night, seemed huge. The vast sky merged into the black mountains, and the radiant stars seeming so close made me feel as if I were wrapped in a black, spangled, velvet cloak.

The mournful chanting had stopped; the vigour and the passion had faded like the dying embers of the fire, to be rekindled another day, another time, in another place. I imagined the porters lying, silent and still, close to one another on the open ground. They'd be huddled in their yak blankets and they'd pull the broad cloth over their shoulders and across their faces to keep warm. And as I imagined them making this final gesture of the night I lay thinking of home, and watched my Great Bear watching me.

At four in the morning, cold rain, coming steadily down, wet our faces and dampened the sleeping bags – and we shot into the tent.

3

Bridges of Fear

THE camp was asleep, apart from a few porters who were struggling to puff life into the smouldering logs from last night's fires. Their efforts were frustrated by the drizzling rain and only the odd coil of smoke drifted up in the misty morning air. It was 4.30. By six o'clock the cook-boys, carrying a large kettle of bed-*chi*, arrived at the tent. 'Hello, Memsahib, tea ready,' they called, and as they passed mugs of milky tea through the door we saw clearer skies coming over.

The rude awakening by the rain had prompted an early packing of the backpacks and we stuffed them with lip salve, sun cream, sunglasses, tissues, throat sweets, Swiss army knives, film, corn plasters, cameras, salt tablets, aspirin tablets, water-purifying tablets, water-flavouring tablets and, most essential of all: a water bottle. The importance of maintaining a high level of fluid intake, to combat dehydration and altitude sickness, was a major consideration. I was still dogged by a gnawing fear of bridges, and that made the breakfast of cereal, eggs and chapattis impossible for me to eat.

We dismantled the tent. The porters took it away and John and Brian fired the starting gun by strolling gently out of the camp with a trailing tail of five or six pensive trekkers, all wondering what lay ahead, in the 110 miles to K2 base camp at 17,500 feet.

A fast-rising sun (already beating on our heads at 7.30) drew the scent from the sage and rosemary bushes. The big blowsy dog roses, all tousled and pink, blazed out from between the boulders. A tiny mouse sped across our path, fleeing from the noisy intruders, and shot under a gnarled old rose root. The thorny stems provided excellent cover.

An hour later, Malcolm, having seen the porters packed and away from camp, caught us up, counted his flock and found one missing. 'Where's Alistair?'

'On ahead,' we told him. 'He disappeared around that hill twenty minutes ago.'

'Ah.' A pause. 'I hope I can catch him. He'll miss the turning to the bridge.'

The words went through me like a knife, refocusing the fear that the pleasures of the trail had blurred. The bridge was obviously nearer than I had thought!

I watched Malcolm striding off after his lost lamb, his *balti*-hatted head down and his umbrella used as a walking stick. He quickly disappeared around the bluff and I began to feel panic.

'Don't you go on too far,' I called out sharply to John and Brian.

'Don't worry, old gal,' John called back. 'We'll get you over the bridge.' Then he added, 'With a bit of luck and a following wind.' He used this expression a lot – to stem fears and rally troops – but it didn't do much for me today.

The path twisted and turned up through terrain of rugged grey rock. It led to a village encircled by irrigated terraced fields of wheat and barley. Sitting under an apricot tree, we drank thirstily from our water bottles, and then pressed on. I, in my nervous state, left my walking stick, which Pemba had given me, behind. Soon we saw Malcolm and Alistair coming back. Malcolm waved and gesticulated at us, pointing over to our left. 'Over that way,' he shouted and pointed towards the edge of the gorge.

I felt my teeth clench tight and a long indrawn breath of fear froze on my lips. We came to the edge. I looked down. We were on the top of a hundred-foot slope. At the bottom of the slope was a gorge, worn smooth and cut hundreds of feet deep by the Braldu river. Lying across it was a log, just a log, with no ropes or sides. Every nerve-end jarred and stiffened as a dreadful sense of impending doom swept over me.

We started down the slope, loose crumbling scree making it hard to control our pace, and we either slid in short bursts, skiing on our boots and throwing up clouds of grey dust, or walked gingerly like Polly and Sue. I slowed considerably as we neared the bottom, having no heart to walk the last two hundred yards over to the gorge. Brian, seeing my reluctance, gripped my arm and walked me along – fifty yards, forty, twenty – all the time his grip tightening a little as we moved inexorably towards the lip of the abyss.

The confrontation was every bit as horrible as I'd imagined – but the inevitability of having to cross was worse even than I'd anticipated. Now I saw that the bridge consisted of two logs, lying side by side, and quite round, about eighteen inches wide and twenty foot long, with no sides and no ropes! It was not wide enough for two people to walk side by side and only precariously lodged on the rock at each end. It spanned a chasm hundreds of feet deep. Brian's hand locked on my arm. My head reeled.

He put one foot, carefully, on the right-hand log, felt for his balance, and shuffled slowly out into space, like a mast on a ship with only sky around him. I stared at him, stupefied.

'Come on, Mags – it's all right.'

He lied, I knew. I test-touched the log with my foot, felt if it was steady; was it firm like a rock? I couldn't go, but I had to. I slid my right foot forward, my body holding back. He urged me on quietly, and as if by some divine means, my foot shuffled forward – a fraction, just a fraction, ready to be withdrawn instantly. One inch – two inches – scraping against the wood. But how could I lift the back foot off the solid ground, swing it forward, and take that first paralysing step? I lifted my left foot, wobbled, and brought it down on to the other log, and somehow started to shuffle along, stiff as a ramrod, with Brian still holding tight on to my arm. It was agonizing progress, as my head swirled like the water beneath me and, all the time, I wanted to go back but then it was too late to go back; I was too far along. I couldn't breathe, felt I was going to be sick. 'Brian don't leave me!' I looked at him – at us both standing in space – and wavered, feeling my balance going, but his grip, like a vice, steadied me, though his voice was pale. He stood sideways, looking back at my feet, willing me to move, and we crawled, inch by inch, charged with tension, along the tightrope, me stiff with fear. Hours, it felt, edging along, till suddenly he moved quickly, hurrying and, with forced gaiety, called out, 'There, we're over – that's it, it's all over!' He stepped on to solid ground, a beautiful, huge expanse of it and yanked me behind him. I staggered, my knees had gone, to a wall of rock, and held gratefully on to it.

There were no words, or control, over my racking sobs, only the sound of Brian trying to console the inconsolable. He sighed deeply, and then he said, 'Thank God you didn't panic. I kept thinking, if she slips, she'll take me with her.' I stared at him, stunned. A trace of a smile lay on his lips, but his eyes were cold and serious. Suddenly my tears felt embarrassing, self-indulgent, and the enormity of the risk I'd let him take only then became horribly clear.

John came across the bridge with Susie, who made it with composure and poise, as did Polly and the rest of the men. They handled it confidently and Ed even danced about in fun – but I couldn't watch that; my fear was too ingrained and it just frightened me all the more. Phobias are a terrible nuisance, and I was a long way from curing mine.

Sitting high up on the rocks, we watched some of the porters, loaded with top-heavy packs, coming over the plank. They treated it with the greatest of respect and, before crossing, prepared themselves by touching their talismans and saying a little prayer.

There was just one small question niggling away in the back of my mind. Now that I was over the bridge, and had become brave enough to talk about it, I said to Malcolm and Brian, 'What about the bucket? I thought we were going to be swung across the river in a bucket on a rope?'

There was an icy silence. I looked at Brian and Malcolm, waiting innocently for the reply, and when I saw that Malcolm was shifting uncomfortably from one foot to another, avoiding my eyes, I realized that something was wrong.

'That was the bridge,' I said positively, pressing for confirmation, 'wasn't it?'

He nodded his head, drew in his breath and said very quietly, 'Afraid not. We won't reach the river crossing with the bucket for a couple of days yet. I just wanted to get you over this one first, that's why I didn't tell you yesterday.'

My heart sank. They looked on in helpless silence and I just wanted to go home.

We swallowed the last of our water and set off again across a wide barren desert area, following a footpath that climbed high above the river. Two hours later, tired, thirsty, and apparently lost, we started to eye the heavy black clouds that were coming over. Malcolm was beginning to wonder why we hadn't sighted the camp when, abruptly, we found ourselves at the top of a cliff. Its crumbling face was eroded by water channels flowing down to the river two hundred feet below. Even as we scanned the cliff for a way down, part of the face cracked and broke away. We'd obviously taken the wrong path, but where were we to go now? The wind blew strongly, pushing the heavy clouds nearer.

Malcolm decided to go back to find another path, and left us with a warning to keep away from the cliff-edge. He lurched down the hill, his body bent against the wind. His voluminous cotton suit flapped furiously around him, and suddenly, diffused in the fading light, he became 'Lawrence' in a silent, flickering movie heroically crossing the desert. He was a fearless leader getting through – and so from then on, we referred to him as 'our hero'. It wasn't long before he was back, his rescue wasn't quite of the heroic proportions we'd joked about, but we were nevertheless glad to see him and hear that he had seen the porters lower down by the river. We headed back after him as the rain started. It was cold and we were glad of our waterproofs. At camp, Razzu and Hussain had tied a tarpaulin up over a wide split in the rocks and made a log fire. We were pleased to see that the kettle was on.

Doug arrived later, delayed by hiring more porters. We now had 188 of them. We were soon pitching tents on a small patch of sand on the otherwise pebbly river bed, and we women made our second attempt at constructing the tent. Having stuffed the rods in all the right places, Polly and I walked around with it aloft while Susie decided which way it should face.

'Would Modom care for a south-facing aspect or morning sun?' we jibed. She prudently chose downwind, out of the rain.

During that evening, which was now fine, Phil Ershler (a high-altitude guide on Mount Rainier) warned us against taking pills of any kind to ward off altitude sickness. Instead, he advised extra fluid intake, believing dehydration to be the main culprit. He also told us not to disregard any possible symptoms, however unlikely, in ourselves or our friends, pointing out that helicopters were few and far between in the mountains. 'This sickness knows no rules – young, old, anyone can fall prey to it,' he said, 'and it can draw the teeth of even the fittest climber. It has done so many times, although it's usually high on the mountain, so the climber's code of "climb high, sleep low" cannot be dismissed lightly. You should drink as much fluid as you can. Drink until it makes you sick, then drink more, and the water you pass should be clear.'

This was sound advice, but the difficulty with it was that good drinking water, surprisingly enough, wasn't always readily available up in the mountains. The advice also had another consequence, which was not only inconvenient but, more often than not, embarrassing. It proved so for me that night. Ever mindful of my experience at Everest, I'd decided to take Phil's counsel and drank four litres of tea and orange squash to ward off a worrying headache that had been coming on all day. Later, I was quite pleased (as the remedy seemed to be working and the headache had virtually disappeared) until nature took its inevitable course. In the night, I was out of the tent three times, which involved the noisy scraping of zips up and down, and me tripping over guy ropes.

In the morning I said that I didn't think much of Phil's theories, and pointed out to Susie what I saw as a significant flaw in an otherwise brilliant remedy. 'So I think we'll have to pitch our tent away from the others tonight,' I said crossly, rummaging about in my bag for my torch and complaining about not being able to find it last night.

She didn't answer.

'Don't you agree?' I said, trying to prompt some kind of response.

Eventually a sleepy, uninterested voice said, 'Why?'

'Well, if I'm going to have to drink litres of fluid every day, and keep going out more than once every night, I can't keep trying to do it quietly near someone else's tent – or looking further afield in the dark for somewhere more suitable. I was up three times last night, you know,' I said crossly, as if it were her fault.

'You think I don't know that?' she retorted. 'I should think everyone knows that.'

'Oh Lord, do they?'

'Yes – of course – the noise you were making – flipping zips up and down and stumbling about. I think you should sleep away from the camp if you're going to carry on like that – then at least the rest of us could get some sleep.'

'Hello, Memsahib; tea ready,' Hussain called through the tent flap.

'Oh no, not more fluid,' I wailed and Polly came in from her night outside.

John's voice boomed through the canvas, lively and hearty.

'Come on, you gals, up. Hot sulphur springs today; bath and hair wash.'

'Oh – wonderful: a bath after six days.'

'Yes – but it's at the top of a twelve-hundred-foot climb.'

We groaned.

'Thought you wouldn't like that,' he said, 'but they say it's smashing up there. Look, Tim wants you up smartish because it's tricky over the sand slides and he wants everyone to be together, so gird your loins quick and get cracking – you're not here to enjoy yourselves, you know.'

Our moods went up and down like the zips, with the day's itinerary: first the honey-coated carrot, which we fell for every time, then the stick, which was a bridge, or a river, or some daunting climb.

'Any blisters to report?' asked Susie, suddenly cheered as the thought of things medical came into her mind.

Phil and Tim acted as a vanguard to take us across the long slopes of scree and grey sand which fell hundreds of feet steeply to the river. Doug and Tim waited halfway down the slope. The first porter to go across left a trail of deep footholes, shifting and mobile. We balanced by leaning heavily into the hillside, left hand plunged up to the wrist, groping for some purchase, while we carefully watched the slope above and below us for any slight shift which could mean half the hill was about to slide into the river. It had happened: a friend of one of the climbers had once triggered off a slide, and it took him with it. He drowned in the river.

Finally, turning away from the river, we found firmer footing and eventually stopped at a welcome stream flowing down an enormous cliff.

'Have a rest here and fill up your water bottles,' Malcolm said. 'We're going up there.'

Our heads turned up, and up and up until they were bent back on our shoulders and we were staring at the mountan disappearing into the glaring sun.

'Now you know why we had to get up early,' he said. 'To get this over before the real heat of the midday sun. We don't want any heat exhaustion, do we?'

Separately and full of resolve we set off, each one having to deal with the long haul in the heat in their own way at their own pace. Susie had gone ahead and I could see her resting already on the steep path, a blue shape against a brown hill. We were all sharing clothes, and so she was wearing my shirt and fingerless gloves to protect her hands from the strong ultraviolet rays. I was wearing Allen's silk socks, to ease the blisters that had appeared after just a day of walking in my new boots, having left my last ones for Pemba, and Polly was wearing her shiny, short, running shorts. We had been full of admiration for Polly when we learnt that she had run two marathons. But now no one was running, and she was struggling hard to get up the cliff. I smiled when I saw that she was being closely followed by an interested knot of porters who were only a few feet away from the backs of her bare legs.

Pemba's words haunted me: 'Step and rest – step and rest', and my heart beat a tattoo in my chest after the first three hundred feet. How I wished I hadn't left my stick in the village before the bridge. I needed it now, because it would have saved me scraping my fingers and nails against the sandy rockface as I dragged myself up, each leg feeling as if it were double its own weight. I would drag one leaden foot up past the resting foot, and on up higher until it finally thumped down, slightly out of control, dreading the next pace. The enervating sun blazed down on my right side, burning my face and bare arms; I felt I must sit down for a while and have a drink. I pulled the backpack round on to my knees. What was this? The bag felt wet inside. I folded my hand over the drinking bottle. It was moist and slid out of the pack too easily. I groaned with disgust as I looked down at it and saw it coated in sticky orange squash. A leaking water bottle – on only the second day. I couldn't believe it. Blisters, bridges, a raging headache, the doghouse tent, sunburn, and now a faulty water bottle. What next, I thought, as I decided to drink what was left in the bottle and cursed the assistant in the shop who had assured me that it had a leakproof lid. Dejectedly, I looked at the bottle, and watched the line of porters and trekkers, half a mile long, disappearing into the sky.

Mountains are deceptive things; they delude you by presenting short faces of cliff, which look like the top. But up there beyond that bluff is another chunk of mountain, and another, and another, and they get steeper and steeper as you become more and more tired. It's a kind of cruel sleight-of-hand trick, but I suspect that if you saw the full pack of cards from the beginning not only would the mystery be gone – but the desire to climb would go with it.

I climbed for hours with some of the porters, who kept me going. We rested frequently, chatted in sign language and shared my glucose tablets. They smoked their eponymous K2 cigarettes, chewed betel nuts, coughed a lot and snorted. I took pictures of them as they adjusted their loads, and they admired my watch with embarrassing regularity!

I was absolutely worn out when we arrived at some small irrigated fields, and since I was learning that up here 'green' means 'village' and therefore 'destination', I was not surprised to see good old Malcolm coming back.

'You all right?' he asked, taking the pack.

'Yes, but so tired and thirsty and hungry; it's six hours since breakfast. Anything for a woman of straw to eat?' I asked hopefully.

He replied with alacrity, 'Yeah, noodles and Branston pickle!'

I groaned and smirked at his boyish ways and he grinned all over his face.

After hours on hot barren rocks, walking into the cool apricot orchard which sheltered the mud houses of Chango village was nothing short of a magical experience. Everything sparkled. The sun filtered through a myriad liquid green leaves and filled the air with rainbow light. It danced on the speckled backs of skinny little chickens and dazzled your eyes, while the sound of the village women chatting and the children laughing lifted my spirits to healing heights.

Consumed with curiosity, the children studied us closely. The older ones, boys or girls, held the hands of little ones and carried babies on their hips. They stared and stared, with doleful Bambi eyes, from immobilized faces. They were fascinated by strangers, radiating an unconscious, inner calm. Dressed in ragged Western-style cast-offs, the original patterns faded, they looked like Dickensian urchins. Brian and John put their Walkmans on the children's ears, dust puffing up from their hair, and it was lovely to see their eyes widen in absolute amazement and their faces beam with smiles. Probably some of them were hearing Western music, through the little earphones, for the very first time.

4

Waterlogged

NEXT stop: the sulphur pools. We couldn't wait. Fortified with food, rest, and secure in the knowledge that the big hill was behind us, we found the walk to the pools enjoyable in the fine weather. The biggest pool was just large enough for six of us and we slid into the soupy liquid and enjoyed the sensual pleasure of a hot, steamy bath until we were all clean, with skin wrinkled like prunes. But we took great care not to disturb the muddy bottom any more than we could help, because the sulphur gave off an obnoxious smell of rotting eggs. An eagle soared high in the sky.

For every silver lining there's a cloud, they say, and in the comfort of the hot pool we hadn't noticed the big dark ones coming across our bit of heaven, at least not until we'd got out of the pool into the cold air. The temperature had dropped dramatically and, as we set off for Askole, it started to rain. In steady drizzle, we plodded uphill for an hour or two, but going slower and slower as Suzie seemed to be running out of steam. Brian stayed with us and we found our way by stones marked with red paint. Earlier in the year, men from all over the world had come up here to run a marathon at ten thousand feet and the stones had been painted to mark the route to Askole. The prize had gone to a porter.

Suzie trudged womanfully on, wrapped up in her waterproofs. Brian, ever hardy, wore only a *shalwar kameze* and open-toed sandles. He had a small rucksack on his back, holding everything he had with him, a few supplies and a bedroll. He believed in travelling light.

A stand of trees up ahead promised Askole and, heartened by that thought, we pressed on, only to be brought up abruptly by an enormous chasm lying between us and the village. It was a long way down and a dreadfully long, wet, way up the other side. It was going to require a major effort to get us there.

A porter, down in the bottom of the ravine, just beginning the slimy climb up the other side, looked as tiny as a fly on the cliff-face and gave us a depressingly accurate idea of the distance involved. When we finally reached the top of the other side, utterly done in, we found him waiting for us. He offered me his stick. Unsure what to do, I declined at first – but he insisted, and thanking him, I accepted it. Now with my second stick, which was sturdy but a bit splintery around the handle, we trudged on slowly to the camp at Askole. We were cold, soaked and tired when we arrived, and pox and pestilence could not have depressed us more than the sight that greeted us: the camp was a flowing mudbath.

Keith, Ed and Mark, standing in the rain with their hands stuffed deep into their pockets, smirked at us from under their hoods. 'What do you think of this, then?' We just sighed. Then we saw that they had put up our tent for us and Polly was inside sorting out the bags. We were very pleased with that. However, the water which flowed in runnels all around and underneath it looked a bit worrying and Polly said it was also wet inside. Susie and I squelched about in the mud and rain looking for stones to lift the bags off the tent floor while Polly mopped up the inside. Later, we couldn't decide what to do with our wet clothes inside the cold tent, so we kept them on and shivered till they dried.

The call for the evening meal was greeted with shouts of delight from the tents. We needed hot food and mentally awarded full marks to the cook-boys who had prepared it under a dripping tarpaulin as the rain continued. For some reason on this night, we had a segregation of the veggies and the carnivores: veggies in the left-hand mess tent, meat eaters in the right and we separated into the two presumably because it was easier to dole out the meals – though nothing was very easy in the pouring rain.

Still shivering miserably, and trying to avoid the drips off the canvas above our heads, we gazed at the visually warming kerosene lamps. They stood on the blue barrels (which were now tables) and burned without heat, but ten or so bodies in down jackets drinking hot soup soon raised the temperature to a comfortable level. We, the veggies, who were mostly climbers, ate rice, dal and okra, and, for those of us who were not familiar with him, witnessed for the first time Tim's gargantuan appetite. A six-foot-five-inch Aussie, and as thin as a spindle, he probably weighed in at only about twelve stone when wet. At twenty-seven he'd made his name as a considerable climber (being the first Australian to climb Everest) and as a talented photographer, and he had all the magnetism and charm of

Crocodile Dundee. That he could wear a well-worn cotton hat, sans corks, with all the panache of our Antipodean film hero just seemed totally characteristic of the man. Mike (Doug's son) informed us that constant refuelling of Tim was imperative and we watched, with not a little admiration, a laudable 'hoovering' of anything that anyone had left on their plates, which was quite considerable as not everyone likes the food and there was plenty of it. Then he cleaned up every last grain of rice from all of the serving pans.

Because of the miserable conditions outside, we stayed on chatting in the mess tent for some time. It was probably the first time that some of us had chatted at all, such is the slow process of knitting together a group of strangers. This unifying act seems to be a guarded and tentative chemistry, probably best fermented slowly, and in this case to be handled with care, as some of the climbers had been unsure about bringing along a group of "support trekkers". When you have a major objective, which hinges on getting things right within the psyche, as well as in the specific space of time, the idea of coping with strangers, who need attention, may not seem to be particularly attractive. But sometimes the enforced intimacy of a mess tent can play a valuable role and we seemed to gel quite well.

Doug told us that he had been negotiating with Heiju Medi, head man of the village, for a cow, since the Pakistani officials stipulated that the porters must be provided with meat on the journey, three goats or one cow per one hundred men. This was precious little by our standards, but equal to their normally low meat intake. The conversation flowed happily along and quickly turned to mountaineering, with Phil and Steve obligingly answering questions from an eager young Mark and Ed, while Tim and Greg regaled us with hair-raising stories of derring-do, courage and fortitude. I, like everyone else, was at first intrigued by this rare insight into a climber's life, but then a disturbing and recurring theme emerged. I found that the stories of extraordinary experiences, cloaked in risk and danger, as well as the fondly-told tales of fun and adventure, were underwritten by one single chilling factor: many of those special companions were not there any more.

I'd started to wonder what forces drove a climber. What made them play Russian roulette with their lives? If it wasn't the summit that mattered, as some said, but the getting there, then what was this getting there – this highly charged flirtation with the angels? Was it simply a recharging of the batteries? Was the charge essential to get them through Mr Mundane's life at sea level and would only

a life-threatening bolt provide enough power? They had no answers.
The enigma remained. Perhaps we would just have to be content to
know that, for them, climbing mountains was the rhythm of life, as
impossible for them to withstand as it was for us to understand.

These thoughts were quickly superseded by the more immediate
worry: rain. Brian took us up on our offer of cover (normally he
slept out), and trying to cram four dripping bodies into the dog
kennel without touching the wet tent walls was no mean feat. Brian,
with his customary carefree and cheerful nature, shoe-horned himself
comfortably into his space. Polly made the best of being squeezed
into the middle and Susie, who was beginning to show signs of her
'medic bag ferreting', as we called it, lay on the edge of the tent, as
I did, against the tent walls.

There were moments on the Everest trip when I thought I'd been
pretty uncomfortable, but now, with Brian's toes up my nose and
only tiny polythene bags between me and the wet walls, and the
added, awful prospect of having to go out in the night in this rain
for a pee, I began to wonder. I watched the water slide down the
tent. It flowed in blobby runs and pinged off the bags by my head.

'Listen,' I said jokingly, 'I know I paid money to do this, of my
own volition, and I think I'm enjoying myself – but don't, please
don't ever remind me how much, or I'll know I'm mad.'

The rain drummed on, but we were tired and I was sinking,
sinking and thinking of the porters outside – and that, however bad
things seemed in here, they were not as bad as having to sleep out
there. I wondered if they'd found shelter. The last time I saw some
of them, they were huddled under a tree by the hedge – but what
about tomorrow? How high? How long? How hot? Did someone
say it was the Jola bridge?

Mercifully, the rain stopped in the night and we were woken by
the Pakistani and the Norwegian expeditions leaving at 4.00 a.m.
The sky was bright blue and, all in all, things boded well for the
day. But by 7.00 a.m. I'd been violently sick. Something, which
tasted of petrol and identified later by Phil as the plastic which the
cook-boys had accidentally melted into the porridge, had caused it.
However, Askole looked better on departure than arrival, and
revealed itself as a beautiful village. As we crossed the polo field
where the Shigar men come once a year to compete with Askole's
men, someone pointed out that this was the spot where Doug, in
the summer of 1977, had waited hours for a helicopter after his
extraordinary lion-hearted crawl down the Ogre with two broken

ankles. On an absail, he had slipped and swung in a wide arc before smashing himself against an ice wall with his feet, breaking his ankles. Chris Bonington, with two broken ribs, and Doug dragged themselves for eight days (four without food) off the mountain and Doug was carried by porters for three days on a stretcher down the Biafo glacier to Askole. Now, with his four broken ribs, he was going back, yet again. For another charge of the batteries?

This morning we were heading for the Biafo glacier, slowly, since it was terribly hot again, even at 7.30 a.m. The lingering petrol taste continued to make me feel nauseous and the diarrhoea had attacked most of us by now. It was beginning to sap our strength and Keith, particularly, was feeling rather weak.

The Biafo glacier is a great swathe of colossal boulders, tossed, jumbled and trapped in moving ice. Its snout has crept across the Braldu gorge and in another millennium or two it will cut it off completely like a huge natural dam.

Malcolm waited for Susie and me, and we began the memorable journey of crossing it with a party of porters continually urging us not to linger. They were afraid of it, and didn't dally for any longer than the two hours that it took to cross it. It was a boulder-hopping exercise, involving scrambling up the boulders, jumping down and clambering around them, trying not to slip on the loose scree or twist an ankle. The rocks were all wedged, pinned or finely balanced by greater or lesser rocks in a chaotic collection lying as a crust on an unstable base of melting ice. Melting is what was heard, movement is what was felt. The solidity was only a façade – an illusion. In fact the surface was undercut by powerful rivers and the boulders were being carried along, by only a few inches each year, sometimes sitting upon ice caverns hundreds of feet deep. Parts of the crust were only a few feet thick and water could be clearly seen below through gaping holes, or it lay in open lakes. The porters hurried past these black spots, making little cairns (a pile of stones) as a guide to other porters, but more as an offering to the gods, hoping they would see them over the sleeping giant safely – knowing he could wake at any time.

At Korofong (black rock), an idyllic camp site of sandy tufted knolls veined by ice-melt streams, we washed our clothes and lazed over lunch. Carolyn set up a surgery and was besieged by a long shuffling line of walking wounded porters. Mostly the complaints were blistered feet (from the short black plastic boots that they are issued) or sores on their shoulders made by the harsh ropes. Some had head- and stomach-aches. They liked to be given tablets whatever the complaint, as they believed that as the pills went down they took the pain with them and therefore any pill would cure any problem. For some of the more complex complaints a placebo would be given and the patient taken back down. Carolyn always insisted on seeing them swallow their tablets herself and was unwilling to give them a few days' supply to take away, as they would happily swop pills with one another or use them as a trade for something else.

Meanwhile Tim, Greg and Phil checked the loads. Susie and I found Malcolm making a harness. We asked him what it was for.

'For anyone who might feel the need for it tomorrow,' he said.

'Feel the need for it tomorrow – why?' we asked.

'Well, nothing really – just one or two tricky bits – before we cross the river,' he said, rather too casually.

We pressed him further.

'Just a little cliffy sort of bit; nothing for you to worry about,' he insisted kindly and continued to slide solid-looking hooks on to thick ropes. It's well known that there's nothing more guaranteed to disturb one's peace of mind than to be told 'not to worry', and Susie immediately began to fret because she was afraid of heights – and 'cliffy bits' sounded high. Personally I thought 'cliffy bits' sounded rather better than 'river'.

In the evening Malcolm took his flute to a sandy rise and, sitting pixie-like by the stream, filled the air with melancholy music. He turned a lot of people's thoughts, I suspect, to home. Later he came to our tent and talked about everything but the 'cliffy bits' in an effort to allay Susie's fears. It didn't seem to work very well though, as she slept erratically all night and at about 3 a.m. insisted on sleeping right up tight against me – just in case Polly might want to get back in the tent to sleep. I suggested we might wait until she did, and then squeeze over to my side, but it had no effect and we both slept the rest of the night badly in one half of the tent.

The next morning was freezing and we shivered over breakfast. I walked the early part of the morning with Phil: Phil from Seattle, Phil with the deep husky voice who spoke very softly; Phil with biceps like half a rugger ball powerful enough for him to hang off a cliff-face; Phil of the Seven Summit climbs with Dick Bass, the fifty-year-old American whom he'd helped climb the seven highest mountains on the seven continents with Steve Marts, our photographer. Phil of the good advice about altitude sickness.

We caught up with Polly and as I walked now with her she told me how she couldn't help thinking about all the famous mountaineers who had trodden these paths since Godwin Austin had explored the Karakoram a hundred years before and discovered Cathedral Towers, Trango Towers, K2, K3, K4, Masherbrum, Gasherbrum and Broad Peak, four of them eight-thousand-metre peaks. 'Think of all those climbers – from Abruzzi to Julie Tullis – who must have come this way, Mags. We're walking in their footsteps,' she said, obviously inspired by the sense of their presence. This sense of communing with her heroes was something she'd been anticipating and it now felt tangible and real to her. Certainly their heavy walking boots had walked this path and maybe their voices do ring in the receiving ear of a climber who worships at the shrine of the mountaineer. But her gods were not immortal and her picture was sadly clouded by the tragedies of 1986. No fewer than thirteen climbers had died in that one summer: Alan Rouse, Maurice and Liliane Barrard, Renato Casarotto, Tadeusz Piotrowski and Julie Tullis, to name but a few who never retraced those poignant steps.

'Would you like to climb K2, Pol?' I asked her. She said how much she really would with a deep longing and she made me think of the little fuchsia which grows, literally, out of the rocks in the mountains. It looks so delicate and seems so frail, but in reality it's like Polly, very tough.

The 'cliffy bit' was a sheer face rising two hundred feet from the raging river. For solid rock path, read ledge; for permanence, read flaky. Parts of the path were broken away altogether and had been repaired with whippy-looking poles that shored up a few crumbling slates, making our faith in them a little bit flaky too. This is what the harness was for. But Susie, turning a pale shade of resignation, refused the harness, steeled herself like the stoic she is and, by avoiding downward glances (and flanked by Malcolm and John), backed herself along the ledge for the hour the ordeal lasted with only a dash of visible perspiration.

From up high we could see for miles across the flat river bed to the confluence of the Braldu and Jola rivers. The young Jola hurled itself down in an angry torrent and, somewhere up there we were told, the infamous bucket bridge swung across it on a wire. But now, it seemed, there was an alternative to the bucket; however, when Nabi informed us that it was 'to wade the river', the Americanism of 'being caught between a rock and a hard place' sprang readily to mind.

'To cross the bridge takes four hours longer and much money,' Nabi said (a levy of ten rupees a porter is charged by the locals, and with a hundred and fifty porters the reluctance to take the 'bucket' is understandable), 'so if we go by the other way, the river, it is much better, if the porters agree.' 'All of them?' I asked with raised eyebrows.

Presumably our OCs, LOs and porters *did* agree and so the party came to the edge of the wide, rushing water. To some of us it looked remarkably like a river in full spate, although we knew it was only a shadow of its spring size.

The porters went in, three by three, their arms locked together to support each other against the powerful flow. The two outside men probed the river bed with their sticks for safe footing, the water up to their thighs, loads bearing down on their backs and fear written all over their faces. I volunteered to go in with an early group because I wanted to get photographs of the girls coming over, and so I hooked into two of the porters. Then I realized that I had totally misread the expression on their faces: what I had thought was fear was in fact pain; the water was indescribably cold. I was completely unprepared for it and whoever said that 'fear and pain concentrate the mind' was right. We concentrated. The river raged and pulled at our legs with great force, pushing us sideways, tottering like crabs, while sharp stones and ankle-twisting boulders shifted and moved under our feet. I could hear the porters offering some sort of suppli- cation under their breath, and hoped that they would say one for me, but I could think only of the pain in my legs.

There were three of these crossings. The second and third were easier, but perhaps when one has been held to the fire once, and survived, one can do it again. I photographed Tim, all six foot five of him, being brought across by two tiny porters, and Brian and Ed coming timorously together, holding hands.

'How did you enjoy that?' Doug asked when everyone was safely gathered on the far bank. I doubt if I need to be too specific about the wording of the replies, especially from John, who had been utterly terrified. Apparently he had made the mistake of not closing his brolly (he always travels with a brolly) and the rushing water had caught it and started to drag him downstream. Obviously he couldn't close it, but − strange creatures that men are − he couldn't bring himself to let go of it either. Luckily his companions held him back and he lived to tell the tale, but the experience had frightened him terribly, the most frightened he'd ever been in all his life he said

Above left: Loaded yaks on their way to Gorak Shep *(photo: M. Hobbs)*

Above right: A simply beautiful Nepalese girl *(photo: M. Hobbs)*

Right: Monks at Thyangboche Monastery *(photo: M. Hobbs)*

Below left: A Tibetan travelling man *(photo: M. Hobbs)*

Below right: Mighty Atom (eight years old) and Pemba about to spin the chilling tales of the yeti *(photo: M. Hobbs)*

Above: John, Terry, Helen and Susie one day away from Everest Base Camp *(photo: M. Hobbs)*

Left: Bridges of fear *(photo: M. Hobbs)*

Above left: Helen grimly enduring
at Everest *(photo: M. Hobbs)*

Above right: Susie having a
lovely time! Note the layers
(photo: M. Hobbs)

Right: Polly on the Baltoro
Glacier *(photo: John Knowles)*

Steve Marts with his cameras and porters *(photo: J. Knowles)*

Razzu our dancing cook carrying a load up to K2 Base Camp *(photo: M. Hobbs)*

Doug Scott and the author in Dassu, where we learnt they call him 'Duss-cart' *(photo: J. Knowles)*

later. At the time I had to smile, because I couldn't help thinking that there was a little touch of whimsy about being drowned by a brolly, but I didn't like to say so.

'OK Doug, so we've walked the plank, scaled cliffs, been soaked through in our tents, forded freezing rivers, survived the porridge, what next?'

'Oh, nothing,' he said 'not really.' He was clearly thinking ahead but somehow there was a slight lack of conviction in his voice. 'That's the worst of it now, kid; it's all over – don't worry.' He continued dressing Mike's badly blistered heel. We turned away to set off again, cheered by his assessment, when he said slowly (he always speaks slowly and gently, without emphasis, and with a Northern accent), 'Well – nearly.'

Our heads snapped back and he stood there grinning at us.

'Maybe – you'll just need a bit of endurance now!'

5

Rivers of Blood

AFTER a day of sickness, between Bardomal and Paiju, Allen and Carolyn went down with high temperatures and fever, Doug slipped and hurt his ribs, and some of the party began to suffer from heat exhaustion. Early in the afternoon, with the camp ominously quiet – an indication of the appalling heat shimmering off the rose-coloured granite plateau of Mount Paiju – everyone went to ground.

The light inside the tent looked cool, green and pool-like, but the incandescent canvas was a perfect conductor for the sun's remorseless rays and heated the tiny space like an oven. We tried not to move. Even the flies buzzed listlessly.

Having arrived, unspeakably drained, at Paiju (11,000 feet) we were not only hot, but sad, because Brian had left us that morning. He had an earlier arrangement to go ballooning in Belgium. The parting hadn't been easy. His 'cool-man-cool' humour, his supremely easy, knowing manner, had made him a pleasure to be with and we had 'followed' him. Now we would miss him. He took with him dozens of letters hastily written by torchlight the previous night, phone numbers of families to call – 'to tell them how it was at the front' – and a porter, who would probably have had to run to keep up with him. With a salvo of jocularities he had gone, leaving a big hole.

I remembered how excited Nabi had been the previous day about our getting to Paiju. 'Only three and a half hours,' he had said (but we had learned to treat estimated travelling times with caution, so we doubted it, doubled it and dismissed the result as apocryphal), 'there will be good wood and good water, and dancing, and I will be making a shave and Shaheed would be making good fill'im.' He also told us that 'there are bears about – and the cow is dead.'

We had asked what they would do now, since they were supposed to kill the fatted calf at Paiju for the porters. 'They will get another one and everyone will be happy – and dancing.' He had laughed out loud at that and shot a glance at Polly, and it was clear that he had taken quite a shine to her. 'We take a different track back,' he had said, 'in-sh-alla – and if the weather is clear and the plane comes in, bonk' – he smacked his hand on the floor – 'we leave the bus.'

We assumed that he was referring to the Karakoram Highway jalopy and were glad to hear it.

The KKH seemed light years away now, particularly as Greg had told us that we were 'still' five or six days away from base camp and finally, we began to understand the scale and the hardship of our journey.

Susie's eyes were inflamed and swollen (from the ultraviolet rays which bounced off the rocks at every angle – lethally undiminished by the thin atmosphere) and we made up pads of witch hazel to soothe them. The soreness made her feel low and so I left her sleeping and went off to see if the cook-boys were making tea. I returned with a brew and news.

A porter had arrived bringing news that caused a considerable ripple throughout the camp. Apparently the Japanese were coming, all four hundred of them, only one hour behind. It seemed like a siege. They duly arrived – an hour or so later, although not four hundred of them. They arrived like ants, streaming over the hillside and everyone was glad that we got here before them, establishing our camp. Watering holes were not only few and far between, but favourite with the porters, and so claiming a patch was important.

John reported back from the warm pools down in the river bed, and recommended them, but by the time we had summoned up enough energy to go to the river we had missed the real warmth (so quickly does it cool down), and so we walked half a mile out across the stony and sandy river bed to catch the last pools in sunlight.

Paiju Peak, turned all pink and perfect in the setting sun, looked out across the Braldu river at a dense range of mountains. They stretched east and west as far as the eye could see. High above the river was a flat rock, jutting out from the bluff where we were camped, and a Muslim porter, graphically silhouetted against the pink bank of clouds edged in gold, was praying to Allah. He faced Mecca and touched his head to the ground rhythmically as he recited his prayers. The haunting sound of his intoning floated magically and unforgettably over the river in the cool evening air.

Just as Nabi foretold, there were preparations afoot for the dancing. As before, it was to take place by a huge bonfire, which the porters were about to put a blazing torch to, when Tim, gazelle-like, leapt up the bank, waved furiously at the men and stopped them – shocking the newly-shaved Nabi considerably. In his broad Aussie accent he said, 'You can't light that, cobber – very bad to use timber – not necessary.' He flapped at them, like a farmer driving cattle, and they stumbled back, tripping over one another in confusion. Nabi looked on dejectedly.

To be fair to Tim, though, as the influx of expeditions depletes the forestation it is hard to justify a bonfire lit solely for our pleasure. Officially we are allowed to use only kerosene, and we did, but the Baltistanis preferred their natural fuel, and if they could, they would squirrel away a few logs to cook with. 'Gas no good for chapattis, Sahib,' they would say, as they surreptitiously covered their little store. Generally speaking, their own use was not excessive; it was the ever-growing number of fires for visitors that really took its toll.

Earlier on, I had been watching a lad cutting the bark all the way down and around a fairly large willow branch of about ten or fifteen years' growth. In a year or two, the branch will be dead and ready to cut, whereas the tree will continue to grow and provide more timber and important shade. Coppicing is a fine, tried and tested method of conservation, especially where there is such a paucity of timber, and better that than total deforestation, as the Nepalese have suffered throughout the lower agricultural terraces. Our expedition leaders were keenly aware of the problem and watched diligently over the porters and others, in an effort to stop the timber being cut. They regularly read the Riot Act over this and the litter problems, and were conscientious about even the smallest amounts of wood, as well as cleaning up our camp site on departure. Many pinpricks make a wound and our bonfire would only have deepened the scar if we hadn't exercised restraint.

Tim's prompt action may have doused the bonfire but not the fire of enthusiasm in Nabi, and he quickly rallied his men. Soon a hundred or more were squatting on their haunches and some used the plastic water cans for drums. The singing began. It stirred Razzu out of his lair. He was got up ghoulishly as before, the sticks curling back his upper lip, but this time he was also dressed as a woman. He had tins strapped to his chest as breasts, a hessian cloth skirt tied tightly round his waist in a wide band and a plate as a bonnet on his head, held on by a scarf tied under his chin. A string of gaudy Western beads around his neck struck a slightly discordant note. He whirled and twirled to the chanting and mockingly caressed some of the young boys by clasping them to his bosom. When he reached the climax of his performance he passed out in the same impressive sort of coma, but as before, in true Thespian style, he was not quite out – and dreamily soaked up the audience's appreciation.

There was no escaping the dance this time for Polly and me, and we were coerced into it by the energetic Tim, Ed and Greg. Malcolm needed no persuading, and I soon discovered that dancing at 11,000 feet, in the dust, is best left to marathon runners or younger, fitter things. They seem to hurt less and I bowed out after a tune or two with bursting lungs and a heart that sounded like a metal detector near a find. While I was still gasping for breath, I directed some admiring remarks to Carolyn about being able to demur so beautifully and managing to stay out of the ring – when I saw Susie grinning hard at me. She had that satisfied 'biter bit' look in her eye and we couldn't help laughing about Polly and me getting our comeuppance. Quite suddenly, the celebrations came to an end: it was time for prayers and the men disappeared quietly into the darkness.

Allen surprised us all, that evening, by taking Malcolm's role as flautist and his melancholy piping set the mood for Malcolm to repeat the Noah poem and talk about his love. We knew he was in love, as he mooned about like a love-sick puppy as soon as we stopped walking each day and, although we girls thought it was lovely to see, we still pulled his leg unmercifully about it. But I was also somewhat surprised when he asked me: 'How do you know when it's love, Mags?' I answered with the first simple reply that came into my head: 'When it hurts,' I told him. 'My mother always used to say: "Love is a two-headed monster of great pain and great joy."'

When we asked him if that sounded familiar, he cogitated for a while, smiled sheepishly and said, 'Then I think I'm in love.'

We roared with laughter, rolling on our backs, because he'd only confirmed what we already knew. But we were pleased for him, as two and a half years previously he had been widowed, when his wife died of cancer after he had lovingly nursed her for seven years. It was late when we put out our torches – eight o'clock – because Nabi had given us the good news that we weren't going on the next day. We needed a rest.

On the sixth day, the trio of washerwomen went down to the pools with the underpinnings, biodegradable soap and shampoo, up through the shady willow camp and down through the stream. This was a nice walk until we saw the cow. It had proud horns, a thin body and big round glassy eyes which looked sideways at us.

Instinctively we stopped in our tracks, wishing we hadn't seen her. This was the porters' meat supply. Somehow it wasn't like seeing a Daisy or a Buttercup in the pastures at home, because one can never quite imagine them hooked up on a rail at the abattoir, and the stark reality of this was much too close for our comfort. An all-pervading sadness hit us as we thought of the gentle, harmless tethered cow, menacingly circled by cadaverous men honing knives, about to be slaughtered. The porters laughed, seeing us shudder, but we couldn't help it. We weren't used to being faced with life's hideous truths, however unexpected, and we hurried on, subdued – not caring to think how the ritual would be performed.

The pools were wonderful, a balm for the aches, pains and lingering blisters, coupled with the delight of being able to bathe away from the men. We wallowed in our baronial bathroom. Carolyn (the vet from Denver – a lovely lady always immaculately turned out, whatever the conditions) was bathing in the largest pool. She explained that she was more than a little concerned about Paul's health. He had paced himself extremely slowly coming up to Paiju (Malcolm staying with him) and had arrived long after the rest of the party. If he was agreeable, she said, she hoped to give him a thorough medical check-up the next day.

It was a silly thing to do, to go towards the stream which ran down through the copse, but the pleasures of the bathing had left our thoughts unguarded and so we headed happily back that way. It was then we saw the river of blood – a crimson, flowing stream. 'Oh no,' we murmured, looking on in horror and sick with the thought of it.

'Thank God I don't like meat,' I murmured, 'I wouldn't want anyone to do that for me,' and we turned back. We went up another sandy slope which we'd been avoiding because it scuffed up the dust into our clean hair and undid in fifteen minutes everything we had been looking forward to for days.

I couldn't stop thinking of the cow, or of Razzu our comic cook with his dull blade, approaching the cow's soft warm throat. It made me wince. Would he avoid her eyes – would the repulsive twitching of her death throes or the blood spurting out over his hands be as abhorrent to him as it was to me? I doubted it, but in my head I could hear the flies buzzing around the carcass and I couldn't shake off my squeamishness till the diversion of a lively game of Scrabble, thankfully, dispelled the thoughts.

Scrabble had become particularly entertaining since Allen, with the pearly-white, Hollywood orthodontist's teeth, joined in. His rather unorthodox, somewhat simplified, American spelling made for an amusingly controversial game, and we enjoyed many heated, but amicable disputes.

Allen and Steve had been having trouble with loss of battery power for the cameras and, with Doug's help, they were trying to negotiate with the porters to go back to bring up a small generator. They were not getting much co-operation; the porters wanted too much money. In these situations the porters have a lot of muscle and can hold an expedition to ransom if they want to. This porter power infuriated Allen. With his own naturally forceful American approach to the job (rather alien to the slothful, sometimes militant, Baltistani men), he felt he was being thwarted at every turn. He, no doubt, had an equally forceful producer back in Hollywood to answer to. 'It's a case of the tail wagging the dog out here,' he said in disgust as he banged down a winning fifty-point Scrabble word. We stared at him in disgust. 'Hey man, these games are meant to be therapeutic, not competitive,' Malc joked. Allen just smirked.

The porters liked Paiju, which was a place of divide and multiply, add and subtract. They divided up the rice, tea and *atta* (a wheat flour) and multiplied the atta by making chapattis. They added the meat and subtracted the porters; men not needed any more left and went back down. This was all very pragmatic and logical, though the distribution of the *atta* and meat caused considerable agitation. The sahibs and the liaison officers officiated. Each porter had his own cloth, on to which was measured (by a hand scoop) his portion, its size related to how much further up the hill he would have to carry. Then he wrapped it up and tucked it covetously into his bag. But if he felt that his portion was not equal to his mates' – or insufficient for the days to come – then sparks flew, along with arms, and a few plain words, and hats were dashed on the ground in protest; all in all, everyone became quite excited. But actually, all this palaver was essential to the ceremony; it was the bedrock of bargaining for our Asian comrades, who clearly felt that bargaining without arguing was no fun and certainly not proper.

The next day, we were back on the track after an extremely sleepless night; I was troubled with a sore throat, coughing and poor respiration. Susie was more than a little anxious to get off before the sun got up. John was puffing a lot and Malcolm had the greatest difficulty in getting up at all.

We walked up several hundred feet to get on to the Baltoro glacier, our glaciated path to Concordia. For five hours we scrambled over boulders and finally diverted off the glacier for the night's camp – only to find that it was dense with tiny black flies. The flies and the heat, at that prettily named site, Lilligo, didn't help our headaches and made us feel quite ill. Happily, the men scouted out another camp site on the edge of a rushing, babbling river which was lively and we moved to it, but the porters stayed with the flies. Things like that didn't bother them.

During supper, while Mike, a craftsman carpenter, was smoothing out the rough handle of my stick, we saw ibex (indigenous wild goats with backward-curving horns) high up on the cliffs above us. So far there had been very little sign of wildlife, because the terrain is so barren, apart from flocks of choughs with their red bills, but the number and variety of wild flowers were legion.

The Pakistani army were quite conspicuous most days, their helicopters buzzing between their military camps in the mountains, and Carolyn told us that Doug had met some soldiers on the trail. She said that they had asked Doug to join them in a meal – as they had shot an ibex from a helicopter! I should have liked to have been a fly (in the sky) at that moment and seen Doug's face – and to have heard his phlegmatic reply to such an invitation. He, and most of the climbing group, were vegetarian – and instinctive conservationists. Carolyn was a vet, and most of them were humanitarian.

It would, I think, be difficult to find a man who leans more gently on his environment than Doug Scott – and that's not because he has spent a large part of his life under canvas. It's because it's an integral part of his character. Tall, lean and bearded, with a hint of the sixties' hippy still about him, he exudes imperturbability and is a past master in the art of the understatement and self effacement. Rimless glasses window a mind that is deeply concerned about humanities and worries philosophically about the meaning of life. He left teaching to be a professional climber – spending much of the time in the Himalayas – but it is a little known fact that it's an organic vegetable garden that will call him off the mountain one day. When his fingers have grown too old for the cold of the mountains he hopes to plough the fields and scatter the good organic seed on the Cumbrian high ground.

We didn't hesitate for one moment to get back to our beds (Pol sleeping with her body in and head out of the tent) after a lot of dark muttering about the eternal diet of dal and rice (*dal-bhat*) which had begun to pall a bit. The lads (as we referred to them) Ed,

Blond Brian, Mark and Alistair made hopeful comments like 'Any chance of a chip butty'. We had a sort of loaves and fishes syndrome at lunch (when we stopped for it) and that meant three or four tins of sardines between us all, twenty or so hungry people. Half a sardine doesn't go very far, and Susie and I particularly found the unseemly grab for the tin unpleasant. I had no doubt, however, that we could overcome this polite trait if we wanted to, but we usually resorted to the tinned Indian cheese and crackers to fill up on. We did have one small chocolate Jubilee bar and a cocktail-sized packet of mixed nuts every day; ships biscuits or trail food as Allen called it. That kept us going through the day and we survived on that. It was adequate but rather boring.

It was the litre-sized plastic cups that bothered us girls more. We hated them. They became quite revolting and deteriorated rapidly. The thing we particularly disliked was the washing of them in cold, greasy water. The problem was that we started our evening meal with a thick and rather glutinous soup, usually mushroom, in them, then the cups would be washed for the cup of *chi* at the end of the meal and it would come complete with lumps of mushroom and smelling of cold, greasy washing-up water and turned your stomach. The porters did their best under the circumstances, but their hearts were simply not in the washing-up. We would have traded anything for a gleaming clean stainless-steel cup, traded even our chocolate bars, which we didn't part with lightly. They had assumed a growing importance in our little commodity market and were one of the highest forms of currency in the trekking camp.

The food and trekking equipment was all arranged by the trekking company and had nothing to do with the expedition. It was generally good, but given the conditions, and the fact of having to move a large party along for four weeks, there were bound to be problems. We accepted that as part of the challenge to our tolerance, but sometimes that failed us. Our small folding stools, for instance, became a challenge as they started to split and collapse without warning under the weight of the men. The attrition rate was one per evening meal, but we soon found the humour in it and began to make bets on whose would collapse on a particular night. As it happened, that evening it was John's. He wasn't best pleased, as it trapped and cut his finger badly, but usually we found it funny and there was always a joke made of it.

Phil had also made us laugh when Susie asked him if he was married. 'Afraid not,' he said resignedly. 'A woman would have to be mad to marry me, and since I don't want to marry a madwoman I don't suppose I ever will.' I thought that was probably how our families saw us – as a bit potty.

6

Masherbrum-Yum

THE twelfth day, coming up to Urdukas, was the hardest we'd had. It was unending hours of punishing, harsh walking, which not only tested us physically, but pushed our mental resilience to the limit: seven hours of laboured uphill climb, almost without respite, almost finished us.

We traversed along the south-facing side of the Baltoro glacier, stopping repeatedly to drink, rest and marvel at the mountains, since now the famed high peaks of the Karakoram had come into view. We discovered that the range of neighbouring mountains made marvellous sounding boards and if we called out loud, our voices echoed over and over again, keeping us in touch with each other along the trail. Continual pleas for a *chi* stop were thankfully answered and we were delighted to come across the cook-boys with the kettle on – a kerosene stove. Allen and Steve had set up the porters for an 'atmospheric shot'. We were watching them crossing in front of a great bowl of mountains deeply covered in snow, when, just as the porters had passed and the cameras were put away, a loud rumbling sound filled the air. We looked up and, to our horror, saw snow rolling down the mountain in a massive avalanche – coming straight towards us. We were standing directly in its path. Panic and confusion followed, and we fell over the rocks, fleeing, leaving things behind in our desperate attempt to outrun it! Inexplicably, I grabbed my camera – and was still clutching a mug of tea when the full force of cold air and spindrift swept over us – then, fortuitously, it stopped. Recovering from the shock in a breathless pause, we looked back to see what had happened, and saw that the millions of tons of snow had been arrested by the high edge of the glacier. Mercifully, it had settled there, and only a fine coating of snow and icy particles reached us. We all went back, trembling a little, joking about avalanches not being something we'd thought about, and had another cup of tea!

No hours had felt as long and as painful as the last two or three approaching the historic camp site of Urdukas, and we struggled wretchedly on, worried about Brian and Keith, who were beginning to show signs of altitude sickness. I drank eight and nine litres of liquid a day at this point, and we urged Brian to drink anything he had left (working on the premise that it was more help inside you than saved in a bottle), but unless one drank copiously at camp where the cook-boys had plenty of good water, one could quickly run short and become seriously dehydrated. Ironically, glaciers are an example of water, water everywhere and not a brackish drop to drink – as they are composed of water creamy with glacial silt and thus unsafe to drink. At times like this it would have been sensible to have had a filtering bottle.

Polly and Ed were going strongly every day, plus Mark, and of course the climbers, but the rest of our little group limped into the camp, a sickly bunch, bedraggled and speechless, barely able to think, barely able to breathe, hardly able to move or understand why we put ourselves through this. Somehow we hauled ourselves up that last fifty feet of rocky outcrop and flung ourselves on to the grass.

Urdukas was the only green spot around for miles. The barren glacier stretched back to the south; a wall of mountains, which included the Lobsang Spire Group and Trango, rose to the west; and endless snows pointed north. In the 1890s the Italian Duke of Abbruzzi left his spoor here, and eventually a prodigious boulder, so precariously balanced that it marked the spot instantly, was carved with an inscription to him. He led the first expedition to K2, and gave his name to one of the ridges on the mountain. K2's presence was almost tangible here; we could sense its nearness, not only in our conversation, but in an all-pervading sense of anticipation, but it was still three days' walk away.

Tim was making a video of the negative side of expeditions, pointing up the litter, which was mostly composed of bottles, paper, tin cans and oil drums. Our climbers always organized a thorough clean-up when we vacated a site and, as with the tree cutting, were aware of their responsibilities in this direction. So it was disappointing to see evidence of the fact that others who had gone before us didn't feel the same, and that Urdukas was liberally strewn with foreign matter. The climbers liked to enlist the help of the porters and encourage them to think clean, but even the promise of extra rupees didn't seem to mobilize the Baltistani men much. The porters' concept of rubbish was not like ours, because for them everything was usable. They sat among the rocks, bemused, watching as Mike dragged the heap of cans, collected in a tarpaulin, down on to the glacier and hurled them into a chasm. In time, they would be frozen into the ice, and one day, aeons later, they'll probably reappear in pristine condition miles down the glaciated road – just as, sadly, some bodies of ill-fated travellers and porters do from time to time.

We were four porters short, since two had eaten some of their meat raw, and were very ill, another had serious head pains and the other fell yesterday, hurting his head. So Nabi (and Mike who'd skipped about like a young lamb with his extra load on the way up) had carried eighty pounds and Nabi hadn't slept all night worrying about his sick porters. He came to our tent to apologize good-heartedly for not looking after the ladies, and said, 'When we leave the climbers at base camp I look after you better.'

On the thirteenth day we girls struck camp in record time – forty minutes – from bed-*chi* to breakfast, and left Urdukas at 6.15. We were to cross the glacier again over to Goro, camp there for the night, and then go on up to Concordia, Throne Room of the Gods, the next day, reaching base camp in three days' time. The previous day we had walked five hours even before the *chi* (and avalanche) stop and we were expecting a similarly long day, with no shelter from the sun.

Stopping to contemplate a little stone-framed graveyard on the edge of the glacier, Susie and I found ourselves looking back long-ingly at the relative lushness of the green oasis of Urdukas. With foreboding, we turned to the paradoxically parched glacier – a vast stretch of boulder-strewn terrain, stretching forever, north-eastwards towards Concordia.

We set off, apprehensive about finding the route as there was no indication of which boulder, or which ridge we should climb, and we were not able to see other people for more than a few minutes at a time. An hour or so later, we were pleased to come across John – perched on a rock under his umbrella – and, I suspect, quietly watching where we were going. As we lay back on a rock trying to still our pounding hearts, cool our brows and justify our motives, he said, with supreme nonchalance, 'A helicopter, back to Skardu, from base camp, would be nice, wouldn't it?' He fiddled with his sunglasses casually, waiting to see what we would say.

Susie shot up. 'What do you mean?'

'Well – I was talking to the Norwegians at Paiju and they have a helicopter coming to fetch them back from base camp – or rather the mother.'

'Why?'

'Well, you know she came out here to see where her son died, to mark the grave, I think, and doesn't want to walk back. She's very upset, naturally.' He put his sunglasses on, slowly. 'It could be quite expensive – but I thought if we catch them up before Concordia I could talk to them about it. They have a radio with them, I know that.' A wry smile crossed his face. 'I wondered if we could arrange something – I wouldn't mind going down in the helicopter and getting back quickly, would you?'

'Oh John, do you think we could?' Susie asked eagerly.

'We'll see,' he said. 'Look girls, I'm with you – we're a team, all together. If ones goes we all go, right. You think about it.' And he pulled on his backpack, flicked up his brolly and strolled off. I didn't answer, hoping I wouldn't have to make the choice. I wanted to walk back.

Goro camp, overlooked by Crystal Peak, was cold. The brightly-coloured thick down jackets that we were now wearing were an indication of the transition from the blinding-white sunlight to the steel-grey cold of the late afternoon up in the snows.

Brian was ill and showing distinct signs of cerebral oedema. Carolyn was concerned. We gathered around him under a tarpaulin near the cook-boys' fire where Ed had him resting. I knew how he was feeling. A pounding head and a frightening weakness brought on by not being able to breathe is profoundly disturbing. Carolyn decided to give him Dexamethasone, a new drug which had only recently been tried for altitude sickness, and incredibly, he recovered reasonably well in a couple of hours. We all agreed that it was good to know that we had drugs with us that could snatch you back from this dangerous sickness as quickly as that. Paul struggled on, though he didn't look well. Carolyn had come to the conclusion that he was basically fit, but that the journey was simply too arduous for him. Most of the time it felt too arduous for all of us!

Slushy snow and water was running all around the tent and Polly scraped out channels to divert the flow a little. Susie was inside fluffing up the nest. It was going to be a hard rocky bed. I sat outside and mended the zips on two of our bags and wondered what the answer would be if they became irreparably damaged. An American, whom we had picked up on the trail, was chatting to me. He was from the Rockies and travelling alone in the Himalayas. He had the deepest, booming voice and that, combined with a wild Gold Rush beard reminding me of a grizzly 'barr', made him a parody of a Klondike 'forty-niner miner' – in the wrong mountains. We were talking about the glacier and it reminded me of the tale of the climber who was camped on a glacier. He was taking photographs when he saw his carry mat sliding away on the ice. Apparently he flung himself on to it, to save it, and it acted like a sledge – and carried him over the edge of a crevasse.

We were also surrounded by crevasses, ice-green pools, submerged lakes and the continual sound of cracking ice. I didn't like it at all, though Susie and Polly didn't seem as conscious of it. I wondered if it was just me hyperbolizing – until about four o'clock in the morning when there was an apocalyptic crack right underneath the camp which frightened us to death. We were sleeping badly anyway – what with rocks in the bed, water in the mats, condensation and cold, so the three old ladies went out to the lavatory, and there, in the pale dawn light, were the porters clustered together in their small stone circles with only their blankets wrapped about them. Their faces were buried in the folds and their knees were drawn up tightly in foetal positions. Their very shape looked cold, and they forlornly faced their pathetic little fires, which were all smoke and no heat. The small sticks, and occasional flame, could not better the thick, wet night air. Only the low stone walls protected their backs a little as they waited for some warming dawn light. They were so hardy, it put us to shame.

But these little lessons made no difference to the morale as the silent column of physically drained trekkers left the camp that morning and began the hard thousand-foot climb to Concordia – through deep snow – until I saw Masherbrum. And then I felt 'it' . . . the mesmeric, overpowering awe of a 'big' mountain. I'd seen it in other people's eyes when they'd talked about 'their' mountains – but to me that sensation had always been rather an enigma and I'd never felt it – till then. Masherbrum froze a moment in my life, a special, magic moment. I stumbled sideways, tripping in the deep snow, unable to release my gaze or drag myself out of its magnetic force – and as we walked on, and on, and on, past this awesome colossus, cloaked in snow, I didn't want to leave it. I just wanted to stay and look and look at it, and I tried to tell John and Susie how it felt – how it made me tingle all over – but they were preoccupied with something else. They were battling with exhaustion, and even, maybe, watching, with justified anxiety, the lenticular clouds blow-

ing off the top of Masherbrum – because lenticulars mean bad
weather, but I ignored the clouds and clung to my new mountain
awareness, and re-named it Masherbrum-Yum.

Susie was extremely low, but she had so much mental strength I
thought she would be all right. Polly was OK because she was driven
by the prospect of going up to Windy Gap, but Ed was beginning
to treat our chances of getting there with scepticism, seeing energy
and time running out. Everyone else plodded stolidly on. Just as Ed
was talking about Windy Gap, and I was thinking of how the
weather rules up here, the sky turned an unbelievable green and
down came a white-out of snow, falling quietly like confetti. And
up went John's brolly, a pitiful shield against the indomitable
elements, but we clung to the smallest crumb and carried on. The
poor visibility only added to the struggle, and on top of hours of
slogging through snow up to our knees at 15,000 feet I began to
feel as if I'd had it. 'I'm not going to make this Concordia place,' I
said every time we stopped to breathe, which was every few steps,
but no one took any notice as they were gritting their teeth and had
their own psychological mountain to climb. It seemed to be more
trying because you had no sense of distance, no means of knowing
how far away the camp was, and naturally everyone was saving
their last drop of strength from their rapidly draining pools for their
own problems. Then Doug appeared out of the snowy greyness,
coming up from behind, and he said that the camp was only just
over the hill which we could faintly see ahead of us. This injection
of hope pushed us over the hill, and there, not a hundred yards
away, shrouded completely in the snow storm, was the camp at
Concordia. It didn't look much – but it was home.

Gallons of tea, food, warmth from a heap of rucksacks and bodies
tightly packed under the cook's tarpaulin restored some of our
spirits, and we watched Mike prepare a flask of hot tea and go back
to bring in the last of the party.

After supper, an icy-cold moon, moving in and out of Rackhames-
que clouds and mountains, lit our way along the snow-covered path
to the tent. We snuggled down quickly, without removing a single
piece of clothing, glad now of the snugness of the small space.

Another snow storm in the morning, blanking out the mess tent,
cast an instant gloom over the dog-kennel spirits, but we found the
spirits in the mess tent even lower. The bad weather conditions had
forced an unexpected decision: the trekkers should stay at Concordia
and maybe go tomorrow if the weather was good. The disappoint-

ment among those who particularly had Windy Gap as their goal
was substantial, while the whole of the group of trekkers, who had
travelled so hopefully towards their objective, enjoying the good,
persevering through the bad, began to think they might not even get
to base camp. The despondent group stared, heartsick, into yukky
mugs of milky tea – and in the kind of silence that speaks louder
than words, I couldn't help thinking of Everest.

Having dealt with the load weighing, allocation and porter paying,
the climbers, equipped with mountain skis, were getting ready to
go. They slid off (carrying huge packs) past the slowly moving line
of porters (most of whom were wearing only their short boots on
bare feet), saying that they might be back that night, or maybe the
following morning – or not at all. Seeing them go off through the
snow, and not knowing if we would see them again only added to
our stock of negative emotions.

Allen and Steve, hurrying up front of the column, filmed the bleak
scene of the porters snailing along like a conveyor belt. Only their
eyes showed as they pulled their blankets up over their heads against
the weather. They were bent low, and the dark, intimidating loads
carried high on their backs distorted their human shape as they
walked away into the falling snow. The head of the line faded slowly,
drawn into the eye of a world which we had yet to see, sucked into
the snow storm – gone. Somehow it felt sad.

One of the problems was that our porters didn't want to go on.
This was not only because the carrying conditions were bad, but
also because, if they had to turn back to Concordia, due to the
snow, they might have lost their stone pens to the oncoming
Japanese. Without the warmth of these little stone camps, in the
wet, they were, understandably, afraid of hypothermia. One damp
yak-hair blanket is not sufficient insulation against the might of
extreme mountain weather.

Mountain weather is a capricious elemental force, and while the
ramifications of our staying down were still being discussed some
time after the climbers had left, the snow stopped, the clouds cleared
– and someone decided we could go on. With a 'Camp Granada'
reaction we were off!

The tent pegs were frozen into the ground, and because we were
anxious to get away quickly behind the porters, Malcolm kindly
offered to stay and get them out for us and pack up our tent. We
left him chipping away with an ice axe. Paul looked on. He had
decided to stay at Concordia and they would try, with the help of

an army telephone, in a camp near by, to get a helicopter to take him back to Skardu.

We followed exactly in the porters' tracks (and to our surprise also a fox's), having been warned not to veer away from their route. But at 15,000 feet, postholing to the top of our gaiters in the raw cold seemed to be just too much, and the ever-expanding elastic thread of endurance sagged a bit when Susie, the mainstay of us all, collapsed in the snow.

Between bouts of vomiting and tears, she said that she'd had it, that she was sick and couldn't go on. I told her not to worry and that we would go back just as soon as she felt able. Typically though, she was concerned about my not getting to base camp. I quickly dismissed that train of thought and reassured her, adamantly, that at that moment there was nothing I wanted to do less than get to base camp, that her well-being was far too important to me to bother about it. If this had been my second chance and it had slipped away, it was simply too bad. There would be another time, another day. 'Perhaps I could be the first person never to get to a base camp.' I joked, trying to ease her mind. 'Don't worry about that', I told her, 'but I have to get back to the camp and stop Malcolm from sending our tent on. Will you be all right if I leave you?'

'Yes, yes,' she said quietly sitting in the snow, so I hurried back, tumbling in the deep snow and breathing like a dragon, not able to think about anything but stopping the tent and having somewhere dry to get her into. I caught Malcolm in time – in fact the tent was still frozen into the ground and he hadn't been able to move it at all.

There is nothing like your own bed when you're feeling ill, even if it is a wet carry mat and a damp sleeping bag under a thin canvas roof. Malcolm and I got Susie back and into bed, and once the sun was shining she began to feel better. The fact that we were not alone quickly restored our equilibrium and, luckily, we had the amicable company of Malcolm and Allen, Steve and Shaheed, who were staying down to wait for the new generator which they hoped would arrive that day. The bush telephone works efficiently up and down the K2 road and so they had good news of its coming up.

Now we had the time to appreciate Concordia, which started to look more like Valhalla as the day wore on. Now we could see why John had wanted us to see it – the point where the Godwin Austin glacier and the Abruzzi glacier join the Baltoro. It was interesting to think about these frozen rivers being the life force of Pakistan, thousands of miles away, to think that when they eventually melted and formed the mighty Indus, they brought all the glacial scree down with them and made the alluvial plains of the Punjab. We were surrounded by 7,000- and 8,000-metre peaks – Mustang Tower, Gasherbrum 2 and 4, Mitre Peak, Chogolisia – and, in the distance up the Godwin Austin glacier, was Broad Peak. It was an opulent display of princely mountains, but K2 is king, of course.

It turned out to be a fine day, with Susie recovering her strength, a good lunch (we chose our own), lots of nattering, an afternoon nap and a cosy supper round the cook-boys' fire under the tarpaulin. Just how good it was we realized later, when we heard of the terrible time that the others had getting to base camp, and we were relieved that Susie had felt ill so near to the camp.

It was on the following morning, day eighteen, cold, crisp and sunny with no threat of snow, when Susie and I came to call at a camp at the foot of Broad Peak.

'Yuu wood like summ garlick saucisse – yes? – urr summ fress caff-ee and biskit – ehh?' purred a French doctor – and we swooned. 'Yes?' he invited again, stroking the words out and slowly shrugging in a characteristic Gallic manner. We accepted weakly. If he had offered us eye of Pooh Bear and heart of Tigger I doubt if we would have refused – we were so overcome. This unexpected caress of the French accent, the sensual timbre of the French voice (brought sharply into focus by the recent lean diet of anything glamorous) was like stroking velvet, or having your hair brushed, or being wrapped in a warm bath towel – and it perked us up immensely.

We'd been on our way to base camp and could find no sign of it after three hours, until we saw a little clutch of tents at the foot of Broad Peak. We wandered into them to ask the way – and to get a cuppa, perhaps – and we found that they were French.

After the initial meeting, we followed them into a cave of tentage and found all manner of goodies hung all over the place: garlic sausage, rich-smelling cheeses, bags of fresh coffee and cushions and *pillows*, and as we use our backpacks for pillows, this seemed like unbridled luxury. The whole place looked like something out of the Sheikh of Araby's harem, so sumptuously was it furnished, unlike anything in our spartan British camp. This unexpected hedonism, in these circumstances, contrasted so sharply with the austerity of the dog kennel that it left us gaping like schoolgirls and impressed. It was just as well that Steve and Allen came by shortly afterwards and reminded us that we still had some distance to go, as otherwise we might have settled down there for the afternoon.

The French pointed out their men on the mountain. 'Zere zay arr yuu can see zhem -on ze left 'and side – fol-low it upp to zur cul-wa -zhere – see.' We strained and strained until we saw two of the tiniest spots imaginable moving across the snow, and we wondered again – why? We wished them good luck and promised to call on them on the way down. 'We don't see too many women up here,' they said, with a wink.

We walked on with Allen and Steve, with a thinly iced cavernous world below us and surreal ice formations hundreds of feet high beside us. Steve told us that also on Broad Peak climbing with the British, was Norman Croucher who had no legs, yet, undaunted, he climbs these formidable mountains. That was another humbling experience.

Allen, a quiet, reserved man, was feeling a little negative. From Hollywood to the Baltistani backwoods was quite a culture shock. What with the cold, the food and the filming problems, he was not adjusting too well or enjoying it much, although he certainly looked the part. Handsome, hirsute, with a thick head of black curly hair and a tidy beard, he was on his first assignment as a director, shooting footage for a full feature movie on K2. But obviously sailing his yacht, and feeling it cut through the blue waters of the Pacific to Catalina Island, was more his style.

If Allen was quiet, then it could be said of the benign Steve Marts that he was only just ticking over on a slow flame, for he said not a word. Steve's illumination came from his smile, a sparkling, captivating smile which lit up the whole of his face. You felt that mere words for him were just an extra that he could do without. We knew that his climbing and photographic achievements were written high in the lists of the great in these fields and, in the credits of Dick Bass's book *Seven Summits*, he writes about Steve: 'He is so totally unique that it would take half another book to convey his qualities and contributions to this odyssey'; but I had a suspicion that you would never learn about them from Steve Marts because he was the kind of man that holds the light for others to shine in and in doing so shines himself. He was clean-shaven; no beard for him, and every two days, just when we thought he was looking even more interesting with his blond designer stubble, he borrowed my old mirror and shaved it off. Then he'd put on his brown leather stetson, smile, and stroll away again – without a word.

Susie and I went slowly for the last two hours, drawn by the towering mass of K2, and experienced a quickening sense of elation as we got nearer to it. Finally, when we walked up on to the spiny moraine (infamously known as 'the strip'), to our Anglo-American K2 Expedition base camp, it was with a soaring sense of excitement.

The cheer that went up as we appeared echoed our own feelings and made all the endeavour, all the hardship, all the struggle with altitude, the diarrhoea, the headaches and the dog kennel worthwhile. The greeting said it all.

Later, when I was looking about me at the few lonely, minute tents lost in a sea of rocky moraine and snow, touched by the heavy skies and the overpowering presence of K2, I wondered again if it was better to journey than to arrive. Being there, however, I knew then that I wouldn't have swopped that gratifying feeling of achievement for any close-run, good effort.

But for the climbers, this was only the beginning. Their journey to the summit started here, with a wait of about two months, setting up camps on the mountain and acclimatizing themselves. Then, with a bit of luck, a lot of skill, indomitable courage and the all-important spell of good weather, they would push for the summit at 28,244 feet. That was nearly another 11,000 feet more of snow, ice, wind, dehydration and endeavour, from base camp.

Polly wasn't there when we arrived and we asked where she was. 'Heading for Windy Gap,' they said, 'with Ed – Doug has taken them.' Susie and I were delighted.

'We had a sodding awful trip up here,' John said. 'Good job you didn't come – we got lost – I didn't think we were going to make it. You should ask Polly about it!'

7

Four Down

WE lay snuggled in our sleeping bags at base camp on our last night, knowing that outside the snow was silently coating the tent and only a thin sheet of canvas separated us from a wild, untamed world. These were cosy, intimate, wound-licking times, as we talked softly at night in the torch's yellow glow. We commiserated with each other over our weak points, laughed at the many good and funny bits, talked about the awe-inspiring sights, reminisced about home, and fantasized continually about the favourite meal we would have as soon as we got there. But tonight we did feel a special sense of achievement.

The evening had been very jolly, the gang all together, sharing a bottle, a song, a joke, and food treats from the climbers' stores, now unpacked ready for their six-week vigil. We had artichoke hearts, shortbread biscuits, Piccalilli, and Carolyn had made a cake. Mike, happiest now because he had 'come home', and hoping to be the youngest man to climb K2, set up his stereo system across the expedition's mess tent. The tent was warm and spacious enough for us all to walk about in, and we had a visitor, the Polish climber Voyteck who was camped down the strip, and who had come up to welcome the climbers.

Susie and I lay thrilled like small children waiting for the bedtime story as Polly rounded off the memorable day with the tale of her trip up the mountain. They hadn't gone to Windy Gap – that had proved to be much too far – but they had gone to the bottom of the Abruzzi spur and ABC and a little way on from there, where they could see Camp One. She told of Ed slipping towards a crevasse and being saved by the rope – and the hair-raising part of finding Keith (dear, dreamy, gentle Keith whom we all liked so much) dangerously wandering alone, on the glacier. He had been keeping the strain he had been under coming up quietly to himself and we had all admired him for that as he soldiered on bravely. 'We just happened to find him – wandering about in a daze – on his own,' continued Polly, holding our fascinated attention.

'What was he doing on his own?'

'You know he hadn't been well, and he didn't want to go with us, because we were all exhausted, and nervous after the terrible walk up yesterday. Then he must have changed his mind and set off without saying anything to anyone. He was obviously sick and lost.' She paused – thinking about what she was going to say, wondering whether to say it at all, then she said tentatively, 'Doug was shocked, then he was furious and shouted, and Keith was exhausted. Well, anything could have happened, couldn't it? At least Ed was roped up behind me when he called out; that was up by ABC, and we turned and saw him slipping towards a crevasse – and Doug yanked him back on the rope. You should have seen the crevasse: it was hundreds of feet down like a great cathedral vault – all green and blue ice – and if we hadn't been roped' – she arched her eyebrows and left the supposition unsaid – 'and then we find Keith out there without ropes. It was really frightening, you know – and so hard to walk on all that ice; you couldn't breathe – we stopped every few minutes. I was so near to tears, a mixture of overwhelming excitement and exertion, I think – but if it hadn't been for Doug we wouldn't have done it; I don't know how they do it themselves.' She drifted off, lost in admiration. 'I can't believe I've been up so far on K2,' she said, smiling and obviously tickled pink, 'it was the hardest thing I've ever done in all my life.'

'It's fantastic, Polly,' Susie said, 'you're a clever girl. We're so pleased that you and Ed managed to get farther up. It meant a lot to you, didn't it? What happened yesterday?'

'Ye-s, what happened yesterday?' I repeated, feeling Polly's excitement with her.

'Oh, yesterday.' She sighed heavily. 'Oh God, that was awful. We got lost.'

'Lost?'

'Do you know how long it took us? Did John tell you?'

We nodded, silently acknowledging that we had heard the time but not the details and that it must have been awful.

'Seven hours. Thank goodness you didn't come. You remember we left late, so the snow was wet, and we were up to our thighs again, every step, and going so slowly that we lost the porters – or anyone who knew the way. Then it got misty or something and we couldn't see – and it was so cold.'

'Who was with you, then?'

'Well, John, Ed, Brian, Mark, Alistair and Keith. We don't know how we happened to find the right bit of path, but after drifting around for ages we saw this high ridge and John knew the strip was on a ridge. Luckily it was the right one, otherwise I think we would still be out there – going round and round,' she said jokingly. 'I was suffering from shock or something, well I think we all reached new heights of exhaustion and by the time we got here I cried and cried – it took me ages to get over it – but Greg and Phil and all the others were very kind and looked after us. They dealt with the tents and things and we had a good meal, and I slept in with Carolyn, in her incredibly organized tent. It puts the dog kennel to shame, I can tell you. She was especially kind to me. I wouldn't have wanted to be on my own after that – it was such an awful ordeal. We were glad you'd been strong enough to go back – that you didn't try to struggle on, I mean. It couldn't have been an easy decision to make. But you did the right thing though. We really hoped you would make it today – we're glad you're here now.'

'So am I,' said Susie, laughing. 'I didn't know how I was going to face Mags if she hadn't got to base camp because of me.'

'Don't be silly, I wouldn't have minded. Anyway, we knew we'd get here, somehow, and everyone's OK, and that's the most important thing. I suppose we've all accomplished something in our own way, via the slippery pole. Just getting to base camp is something for you and me, Sue – and Polly has stood on the Abruzzi spur on K2 and communed with her heroes. You know, Susie and I get a lot of vicarious pleasure from that, Polly. Well done, gal – we're proud of you. Next time the top, eh?'

She smirked and said, 'All I know is I've touched K2, and it has touched me.'

'Look, how are we going out for a pee in this snow?' Susie asked peevishly. 'It's horrible out there. We'll have to get out boots and everything on.' She tutted and groaned.

'Oh, use a pot or something,' I said. 'Use one of those revolting mugs. That's all they're good for, anyway, horrible things. We won't tell anyone, and we'll keep it in here!'

How our kernel of dignity was cracking, I thought, as we settled down to a sleep of tired contentment. Tomorrow, I realized, with a tinge of sadness about leaving base camp so soon, that we'd be on our way down to the relative benignity of the villages again.

But the Karakoram hadn't done with us yet, and it seemed that the continual drip on our stone of strength was at last making its mark. Malcolm (we learned in the morning) had gone into a fit of hypertension the previous night, and John couldn't move – his back had gone. But that was joy unconfined for Susie, and the medic bag-ferreting had begun in earnest as she swept about the camp like an angel of mercy. She was happy. Unfortunately, however, all Susie's doctoring and Doug's massaging (he had an extensive knowledge about preventive and homoeopathic medicine) didn't do much for John's back; it would need rest and not the hours of hard walking that we had in front of us. The only immediate answer was pain-killers, and so we prepared to leave.

Just as we left, we were given a packet of shortbread biscuits, treasure indeed, and after an emotional farewell and an abundance of best wishes and good-luck messages, we trekkers and the film crew left to go back to Concordia.

This time, we took longer than ever to wind our way back along the uncertain ice path. Susie and I stuck with John and 'the back', and Keith. This time they sent out a search party because we were so long; just as John was about on his knees, we saw them coming: Malcolm, of course, leading a group of porters armed with tea, blankets, ropes and smiles hove into view. They whisked away the backpacks (and my camera) and carried John gladiatorially into the Concordia camp. A porter walking beside him held the brolly over his head. Naturally we females and Keith walked three paces behind, but I longed for my camera, 'my kingdom for a camera,' I called, such was the scene – straight out of the Raj. The porters laughed and smiled a lot about it all. You could just see what they were thinking about these silly English, and others, who came away from wonderful countries with cars and comforts in their homes to walk and climb, for pleasure, higher in the ice-covered mountains than any daft goat or shepherd would dream of going – to places where only the army go to snipe at the Indians on the border. It was all quite beyond their comprehension.

At last we had a perfect evening in the mountains, in Concordia, when cloaked porters stood black against a golden-red sunset – and later, in an indigo sky sequinned with stars and the Great Bear, a nearly full moon floodlit the majestic snows of the great peaks. It was a mountain paradise and I longed to see Masherbrum again. But it was also a melancholy evening meal, and a glum group. We missed our friends. After two weeks of their affable camaraderie and moral support we felt a bit lost. We had been through a great deal together.

The next afternoon and evening (at a new camp only a few hours' walk from Concordia) were also perfect. We spent them playing cards (Allen and Ed winning), having a better supper than usual because Nabi had procured some beans from the Japanese, hanging our washing on the longest washing line in the world (the army's telephone wire to Skardu) and climbing up a little to see the most spectacular, blinding sunset we'd ever seen in our lives. All this – and getting the BBC's World Service on John's radio – was sheer delight.

There hadn't been any chance of a helicopter for us, and we weren't even sure when Paul would get away. (He was still waiting at Concordia when we left). So I was especially pleased when, while we were camped at Urdukas, rejuvenating ourselves by its gurgling streams, Susie remarked on how lovely it was to walk back. This is probably because the ascent can be so gruelling that it veils a lot of the many delights which can only really be fully appreciated when fatigue is not a problem, and, of course, the satisfaction of having reached our goal would surely double the pleasures of coming down.

It was so beautiful there. The butterflies danced on the wild flowers and spiders span webs from one rock to another. We lay in the grass, listened to the choughs, drank the cinnamon-peppered tea – and Malcolm got a letter, a love letter. A porter had brought it up from Skardu. Malcolm was ecstatic and we were envious.

The following day we travelled all the way down to Paiju. It took nine and a half gruelling hours. We didn't have a lunch stop and we had only our chocolate bar and nuts to sustain us. We were not happy campers when we arrived and we threw ourselves down in the copse where the cow had been killed. The evening meal preceded vehement demands for a proper lunch stop the following day, if it was going to be as long, and the lads didn't want just dal. Allen and even Steve had something to say about this and then Shaheed (by profession a portrait photographer to Lahore's society ladies) said in jest, 'Oh come now, if you live in the mountains then you have to learn to live like a pig.' This made me smile, as I realized that all this was a fairly dramatic change for the urbane Shaheed himself and that the indigenous population of elegant towns like Lahore normally wouldn't dream of travelling so far up in the mountains. They'd leave that to daft foreigners.

There was no Malc or Allen lulling us off to sleep with a sonorous tune on the flute on that particular evening. But I wondered if John heard our shrieks of laughter later – when we'd got over the shock – at Polly asking us if we'd noticed the brown mug going round with tea in it. The colour drained from our faces as we drew in a sharp breath. 'Oh no!' we breathed quietly. 'Sugar,' Susie said, uncharacteristically, 'we forgot all about it. I suppose the porters picked it up from the tent. How embarrassing! Too late now to say anything about it. Just remember to refuse it if it comes to you.'

'But how will we dare pass it on?' I whispered.

Late in the afternoon of the next day, we arrived at the Jola Bridge – or 'bucket'. The porters had made camp there to allow us to get an early start on crossing the river in the morning. Susie, Keith, John and I were extremely tired and a bit fractious after some pretty serious and strenuous rock climbing and we were surprised to find that there had been a few ructions in the camp. Polly, sitting bathing her feet in a stream, surrounded protectively by Ed and Brian, was tearful and upset. We learned that she and Allen had clashed horns in no uncertain manner. He'd made some reference to her 'reptile skin' and she was still seething with indignation and quite over-wrought. It reminded me of another aspect of strenuous trekking. The physical conditions are hard on the face, particularly the female face, and we had all weathered dramatically. The skin gets toughened and blisters and peels badly and whereas one's 'face dropping off', as John calls it, has a certain macho charm in men, it's not particularly attractive in women. And the spat had come from an unthinking comment by Allen and an over-sensitive reaction by poor Polly, who was already struggling with a cough, a cold and women's things. It is not uncommon, this kind of spark, and it's surprising that it doesn't happen more often with a group bound together in different conditions. It's a credit to the leaders and their general organizational ability to be able to keep a group happy and safe through it all, and ours had been a good, harmonious experience. But with the best will in the world the balance gets a bit out of kilter sometimes. As usual, however our cathartic, psychological philosophizing in the dog kennel at night worked wonders, and we woke in the morning with the steel in our back toughened. Polly was determined to think positively about Allen; Susie suppressed her increased loathing of the *chi*; I struggled with my fear of the bucket.

It hung from a hook and pulley on a steel cable, and lurched jerkily off the rock, launching its passengers, two at a time, into the air. Swinging along like cargo off a ship, it creaked along the cable and eventually banged into the opposite bank, where the porters who cranked the winch caught it, along with its passengers.

But I was braver, more prepared now – and I had no choice. I felt like a terribly pampered nuisance, as everything stopped to get me in the bucket. I clambered up on to the big rock it was resting on and John and I got in looking like Andy Pandy – without the wave. White knuckles gripped the sides as we swung out over white water.

'Don't look at the workings of this thing,' I told myself, tight-lipped. 'Don't even think about it – don't look at the river – good God, don't look at this ancient fruit box we're crammed into, O-o-h, – look at John – no, don't look at John – he looks panicky – look up – oh, no – the wire – the hook looks rusted – I hate the way it swings in an arc – O-h, on and on creaking, swinging – then BANG – into the rock – hands grabbing – voices shouting – legs wobbling, guffaws and hats waving from both sides of the river. I was shaking but felt wonderful. I'd got over in the bucket – and I think I quite enjoyed it – when it was over!

We were all over the river by 7.30 and cracked on at a good pace to the snout of the Biafo. This part, as we expected, was slower, and we'd been watching over a dazed, still silently suffering Keith, making sure he didn't wander off in the wrong direction, as there was only the merest hint of a path through the boulders for the sharp-witted. We also watched over Shadid, who was limping badly with the pain of swollen knees. We thought, having got off the Biafo, that all the hard part was behind us, and we were just congratulating ourselves for making good progress when John went down with the sickness. He had a soaring temperature, was soaked in perspiration and, after being helplessly sick for twenty minutes, was too weak to walk. We got him to a stream, where he lay shivering and complaining of the cold even though the sunshine was ferocious. Then Polly was overcome with it. Some time later we managed to get them to walk, slowly with help, and reached the lunch camp. There we found Malcolm and Keith, also afflicted. They were all running high temperatures and sank into a heavy sleep after we'd settled them down in the ruins of a shepherd's hut which the porters shaded with a tarpaulin. It must have been a hundred degrees under it, but our intrepid friends, previously so strong, were now prostrate.

Susie, Brian, Ed, Mark and I ate the lunch we'd demanded yesterday (which of course was huge, but no doubt the cook-boys enjoyed it), and tried to make contingency plans. Everyone else had gone ahead. Somehow we had to carry the extra backpacks between us and get four sick people several miles on, over difficult terrain, to Askole.

It must have been two or three hours later, after we had woken them because of threatening rain and persuaded them to walk on, that Malcolm went into hyperventilation. It was almost too much. Susie was afraid he was going to have a heart attack. We all thought he was going to die.

Somehow we made a stretcher for him, and Brian, and Susie and two porters carried it. They shambled along slowly, a few yards at a time, and we were all terribly worried. I took extra packs and helped Keith. John and Polly helped each other and Ed shot off hotfoot to Askole for help.

Eventually some porters came with a *charpoy* (rush bed). They lifted Malcolm on to it, but he wouldn't be moved any more. It was as if he felt he was going to die. We sat with him – a confused group of people surrounded by miles of wilderness – ministering over a man we thought might be about to take his last breath. But as the time passed, Nabi persuaded him to be carried to the village and soon we saw Ed coming back with a group of men. He'd found a Basque doctor, and his climbing companions, and they had brought a medical chest along. Malcolm's temperature was over a hundred degrees and there was infection. The doctor gave him an injection to stop the hyperventilation, and antibiotics for the fever. Seven or eight porters took up the bed, which looked frighteningly like a bier, and carried him into the village.

We made plans for his care throughout the night and Allen offered to give him his midnight tablets, prescribed by the doctor. Susie was to give an injection at 2 a.m. By the time we went to bed Malc's temperature was down, Polly's was up, Steve Marts had the fever and Susie thought she was getting it. The others had recovered quite well.

At one o'clock in the morning John was wandering around and Susie was ill. They told me to take a sleeping tablet and get some sleep. 'One of us needs to be rested in the morning,' they said.

Elysian Fields Forever

I T was Malcolm who was rested when dawn broke. He was out of bed! Better! There he was, grinning all over his face and feeling fine, while we of the half-open eyes felt terrible.

He spent the day playing chess under a tree, laughing, chatting and drinking with the porters while the rest of us, worn out, spent it trying to recoup some of the energy drained by yesterday's events.

John and I went to see, only to *see*, Askole's unique bridge. It was the most extraordinary construction imaginable, made of twigs. The ropes, or cables, a hundred yards or more long, were woven in pliable willow. It spanned the river in a deep arc and was anchored way back on the banks by massive boulders. The cables, for the sides and walkway, were plaited, braided and twisted together so intricately and tightly that they formed an immensely strong and durable bridge. It was a masterpiece of engineering and ecological sense, a perfect example of living within one's own environment.

Across the gorge from Askole was another small village almost buried in vivid green wheat and the locals crossed back and forth over the bridge. It was a long crossing because the deep arc meant they had to walk down to the swaying nadir and then climb the slope up the other side holding on to the rough twig ropes – probably carrying a loaded *doko* and even an animal. But Askole was the core village in the area, with five hundred people and a school, and the neighbouring villagers had to come to it for trade.

The bridge was only one of the delights of Askole. We found more when we visited the houses with Allen to buy a hat or a blanket, or beads or shoes, as props for his film company. These houses had a cattle manger dug half below the ground and a floor above. They were simple, mud and stone walled, with no windows and an earth floor. On the roofs, which were flat, the grain was dried and also the dung, which was religiously collected for fuel. Although this semi-troglodyte existence may have looked uncomfortable from the outisde, it had a warm, cosy, humanizing atmosphere inside. It was full of comforting fundamentals like a sweet-smelling log fire with potatoes cooking in the ashes and a kettle boiling to make cinnamon tea. Babies, or cats, slept by the fire in hand-woven baskets. The beds looked inviting, with piles of blankets thrown on them, and not tightly made like ours, as if they were out of bounds during the day. The corn hung up to dry beside apricots, apples and walnuts, and the farming tools leant against the wall beside a small hand loom. Goats and kids nestled in the hay. Chickens scratched at the floor while a cock crowed proudly on the fence post outside. There was a warm, comfortable sense of well-being and the generous welcome of the families pulled at something deep down inside.

The children's school was in the same field as our tents and the classroom was marked off from us by white-painted stones. They carried their little chalk boards to school on their backs. We were discouraged from photographing them at school, because during the climbing season expedition after expedition camped in the field, and so the distraction would be continuous.

In the morning, as we left Askole, the children were singing and they clapped the rhythm with the same downward action as the porters used during their dancing nights. Their happy, bell-like voices faded into the air as we walked through the labyrinth of houses and out of the village. We passed the outer fields of potatoes, peas and radishes which demonstrated the efficiency of their ingenious irrigation system. The water came from the eternal mountain snows, flowed merrily along hand-hewn tree trunks, turned the watermill and flowed on through the fields in split bamboo canes which could be directed into any field at any time. A fragile eco-system hacked out of the mountains by hard toil and one which barely fed its farming communities. It was medieval, almost biblical in appearance, and very beautiful. It was impossible not to feel a pang of loss as we left in all behind.

The sunlit Elysian fields softened the granite mountains as our porters picked canary-yellow roses to put in their hair, and in ours. We were taking a different route to avoid the plank bridge, and the porter's singing, as they trotted jauntily along the road to home, made it an unforgettable day – a celebration of the magic of the Karakoram. I found myself hoping that it would never change – that it would remain Elysian fields forever.

We met other people coming up; Steve Razzetti met his pal Stephen Venables (who went on to be the first Briton to climb

Everest without oxygen), on his way up to K2, and a group of French men who were going to 'cycle' down Broad Peak and balloon off it! We also met a group of Cambridge lads going to study the 'sex life of the willow'! When we said that they were too late, because the willows had 'already done it this season' as the path was a carpet of willow seeds all the way from Askole, they admitted that their study was really an excuse to pay for their attempt at the record for the longest stay on a glacier. This seemed just about as bizarre as their first reason and confirmed my suspicion that the world was full of crazy people doing incredibly eccentric things in fantastic places.

Lower down, in a village, when we asked some porters what meat they were eating, and illustrated the question with a few 'Oink Oink's' or 'Moo Moo's,' and some horn actions, they laughed so hard – because the Nepalese laugh easily – that they couldn't eat it and we laughed with them, because we were very happy. Finally we left the sweet wheat fields in this land of rugged, piercing beauty and tripped through a carpet of wild flowers, to a narrow neck of the Braldu river, where we crossed over in another smaller bucket, and then on to the last camp site. It had taken fourteen days to get to base camp, including rest days – and six to get down.

John, Susie and I sat on a rock watching the sun go down, waiting for the full moon. We reflected on the extraordinary, unrepeatable experience we'd just been through together – and thought how, although the whole party had been harmonious, we had grown much closer during the return journey. It is surprising how long it takes to unite people, and some of the party had struck up special, permanent friendships. One in particular that we thought most unlikely was that between Brian and Ed, who'd seemed so different. But there it was, and to celebrate our last night they surprised us (and themselves, I think) by entertaining us, totally ad lib, from a large smooth rock, which made a perfect stage, by doing a couple of song-and-dance acts, for the first time together – brilliantly.

Our last night in the mountains. There was another day's walk tomorrow but the jeeps would be waiting at Brianso to take us to Skardu. We decided to sleep out, on the same flat rock, and as we chatted from our sleeping bags in the warm night I waited for the moon, which should have been full, and for the Great Bear to show. But a blanket of cloud hid the moon and the Great Bear didn't show. Two days later, we were due to leave Skardu by plane, but it didn't show either, and so we went back down the twisting

Karakoram Highway, vitually non-stop, for twenty-four incredible hours in the bone-breaking bus!

It rather summed up our whole journey: rugged, exhilarating and enlightening. Most of all, though, it had been a visual feast.

Paul got off the mountain safely in a helicopter. Allen's film was much appreciated by the film company and it is hoped that it will be made into a feature film some time in the future. The climbers had six weeks of bad weather and were unable to get to the summit. K2 was not climbed by anyone that year because of the heavy snowfalls throughout the summer and high winds during the autumn – and Malcolm got married.

PART THREE

1

K2, Now Makalu

JOHN said, 'This is the one: Makalu.'

'Now are you sure? This one isn't on the tea-house-trail, is it?' I asked.

'No, it's not, but then that's not what you really want, is it. You *want* to be off the main track don't you?'

'Well . . . Yes, of course, we do really . . . but.'

'No, Makalu is definitely not tourist trail. In fact, it needs climbing permission, and trekkers have to be with an expedition, even though it's still quite close to Everest – about twenty miles east – I think.' He watched me mull it over and added cheerfully, 'You'll be all right, you will all like this one. It's a good time for us: August/September. Nepal's much softer, not barren like the Karakoram; lots of rhododendrons and wooded mountain and villages – really nice.'

'What will the weather be like then?'

'Should be good, and there'll be another chance at a twenty-one-thousand-foot peak – if you're interested.' Then he said, quite incidentally, 'Well, it might be a bit wet – late August, September shouldn't be too bad though, we won't need waterproofs!'

So we decided, after considering various other options, and talking to people who know about these things, to go with the British Makalu Expedition, again led by Doug Scott.

Some days later I said to Helen and Susie, 'OK, this is it – this is finally it – I'm not coming home till I've been to India – even if I have to go on my own.'

'Not likely, Mags: if one goes, we all go. Makalu first, then the Taj Mahal this time.'

Thirteen months after K2 we touched down on Kathmandu's runway with ten other trekkers. It was the middle of August, and the monsoon season. As not one of us had any real comprehension of what that meant, other than it would rain in short bursts during the day, it was a happy, excited party which set off on the journey.

This time, Susie, Helen, John and I had psyched ourselves up into having a crack at the 21,000 foot offer and were armed, artlessly, with ice axes and crampons. Helen, of course, carried her compulsory armoury of earrings but Susie and I were astonished to find that, this time, they were accompanied with a selection of shoulder-padded T-shirts – all glittering and glowing with sequins and diamante. 'For India,' she said. Strange bedfellows with ice axes and crampons, we teased – but, of course, characteristically outré of Helen.

The esoteric term for 'Advance' Base Camp is ABC, and it's considered a bit of a joke to use that term if you haven't been to one, but we disregarded that and told everyone we were going to Makalu ABC, and then maybe on to 21,000 feet. By now our families and friends were beginning to look upon us with the merest tinge of envy at seeing pictures of some of the sites we'd been to, but that was largely over-shadowed by curiosity and total incomprehension. 'If it's hard and terribly basic, with boring food and no showers and everything, why do you keep going back? – You must be mad.'

'Yes, well that's what Doug always says – it *is* a form of madness really.' But so much of it is wonderful, and you never know what's going to happen next. I think that's what we're hooked on – the uncertainties, you just never know what's around the next corner.

In Kathmandu we clambered out of the taxi and clattered into the Narayani Hotel, Patan (in the old part of the city) and walked right into Greg Childs, from the K2 trip.

'Terrific – what are you doing here – are you coming to Makalu?'

'Yes.'

'Great.'

'How will the weather be?' we asked.

'Oh, fine I guess,' Greg said, furrowing his brow as if he wondered why that would be relevant and reminding me that only 'mountain weather' concerns climbers – not walk-in weather.

'Good,' we all chorused happily.

Greg looked extremely fit. He must have been climbing a lot of mountains I thought, and later, when we were having a drink, he introduced us to his friend Simon Yates, who was also coming to Makalu. Later, John told us Simon's phenomenal story. He had been climbing with Joe Simpson on Siula Grande in South America.

During the climb Joe Simpson fell, breaking his leg, and while Simon was trying to get him off the mountain, they both fell again – but Joe fell into a deep crevasse, leaving Simon holding on to him on the rope. After hours of waiting for some sign of life from Joe, and agonizing over his options, Simon, without any means of assuring himself to the contrary, could only presume that Joe had died – and so he cut the rope, having no alternative. Joe Simpson, who was lying with his leg broken, on a ledge, in the dark, eventually, with super-human power and an indomitable will to live, spent five days in agony, dragging himself out of the crevasse, without food or water, and across unmarked terrain back to the camp which he could not even be sure would still be there. Happily, Simon, in his distress, had not moved on and Joe lived to tell his remarkable, heroic tale in his book, *Touching the Void*. And here was Simon, going back for more.

The expedition planned to climb the west face of Makalu, the highest and most technically difficult unclimbed face in the world. Makalu is the world's fifth highest mountain, forming the eastern shoulder of the mighty Khumbu massif. Parts of Nepal's traditional lifestyle are changing due to the tourist trade and there are well-trodden routes to Everest, but Makalu, in the east, is still relatively untouched by Western influence. This was the aspect of the project that appealed to us.

Being back in Kathmandu brought on a rush of blood to the head and a rash of travellers' cheques to the money changer and we girls set about a crazed shopping whirl for the best part of two days. We were quite familiar with the city by now, and Helen sallied forth, brandishing the wallet, with Susie and me trailing in her wake. We marvelled at her astonishing photographic recall of the tiniest difference between this bracelet and that one; or that dress or the other scarf – in every shop in town! After making a considerable contribution to the balance-of-payments deficit, via the silk-frock shops and Tibetan-jewellery stores, we met up with John in the English tea shop. By now Susie and I were gasping for a cup of tea and a break from Helen's voraciously acquisitive *tour de force*. Here, Helen showered him – and other people at surrounding tables – with all her purchases until even they became infected by her contagious enthusiasm for shopping.

Fortunately John quickly brought us down to earth and made us go and buy brollies. He and I also bought a couple of lightweight plastic macs, easy to carry – one green, one pink – to go over our mountain gear.

Eating curry and drinking cheap Indian beer is as good a way as any of breaking the ice in a group of strangers. It oils the tongue, burns the palate, and brings up the wind of even the most polite strangers – and these epicurean vagaries soon disperse any trace of inhibiting decorum. Only the most urbane of happy campers can remain reserved through one of these meals and, luckily, we all seemed to be possessed of a similar sense of humour – which was fortunate, as a sense of humour is vital in these ventures.

Andy Norris was our trek leader. He was a professional photographer and adventure travel organizer with considerable expedition experience. We had five women and nine men. Reg Dacey, a physicist, was the eldest at fifty-six. Spanning the forties were us four and Joan Lancaster, specializing in preventive medicine; Joy Thompson, in business management; and Nigel Toothill, a captain in commercial shipping. In their thirties were Steve Thomas and Peter Judd, in computers; Peter Crompton a teacher; Andy Watts, a physicist; and his big buddy (literally), Simon Brunnen, an electronic engineer. The only teenager was Bryan Robinson, who was 'ner but a lad' at nineteen, teenager thin, with skin as smooth and pale as an oyster and a thatch of blond curls to match.

On our second day we had an important trip to make to the cemetery in Kathmandu; since we'd made our trip to Everest, Mike Cheney had died. His sister (whom we knew well in England) had asked us to visit his grave. We went to the British Embassy and they directed us to their locked graveyard, which was kept by a gaunt old woman who lived in the gatehouse. By now it was raining heavily and so we gladly accepted her invitation to come into the bothy, where she placed cardboard on the mud floor to keep our wet feet off it. John, being the only one with a brolly and mac, went alone to the grave and reported back that it was marked by two trees with a wonderful view of the mountains and that somehow it was meaningful in its simplicity: just the way Mike would have wanted it.

Mike Cheney was known throughout the climbing world for thirty years, having gone to Kathmandu as an officer in the British army and settled there. He had orchestrated many of the great expeditions from his home and travelled endlessly through the Himalayas. He wouldn't have wanted to be laid to rest anywhere else.

John hailed a motor rickshaw to get us back to the hotel but although it was built for only two passengers, the driver insisted we all get in. As we were anxious to stay out of the rain, we did so. It wasn't fast, 'not as fast as a lawn mower,' John remarked, but we might just as well have been on a switchback. Riding in a vehicle tipped at forty-five degrees, cracking one's head against its metal framework as it stopped on a sixpence, and being plunged forward and shaken like a collection box was just another experience in this bizarre, unique world which never failed to provide surprises. We arrived in a dazed state and determined not to take the motorized vehicle again, preferring its human-operated counterpart.

We spent hours repacking our kitbags – this for India, that for Makalu and so forth – but we also remarked on the dramatic change we felt we had undergone since we first packed, very anxiously, for Everest and K2. We felt rather more experienced in trekking now, veterans so to speak, we said, and made the mistake of saying so to Helen, who only too readily agreed. 'Veterans all right,' she said as she pushed her ice axe and boots into her kitbag, and quickly returned to folding her silk frocks into sheets of coloured tissue as soon as we discussed who should carry the nasty spiky crampons.

On Wednesday 17 August we were back in the now familiar small-airport chaos of Kathmandu, where things seemed extremely relaxed, things like ticketing, toilets and departure times, until you wandered off to find a postbox, by walking around the outer buildings in the direction pointed out to you and then things became electric. The previously relaxed, smoking, smiling, rifle-carrying militia visibly bristled and indicated quite clearly that you were out of line.

However, the authorities wanted us to get on, so they weighed our bags and our bodies, then refused to let us go. Our luggage, and we, were overweight. Andy Norris, Greg and Sharvati (Sharu) Prabhu (who had climbed Jitchu Drake with Doug and who spoke Nepali) took on the airport officials and the dispute began. We settled down on the floor while she handled the officialdom, and surreptitiously started to put on any heavy things we could, such as walking boots and heavy jackets, and we carried our cameras instead of leaving them in our hand-baggage. The rest of the climbers had gone on ahead with the bulk of the gear, and Doug, who had seen us off in London, was due into Kathmandu on the next plane.

Joan, a very friendly, chatty woman, was researching the physical effects of altitude and was intending to keep records of our weight, heart rates and respiration. We therefore took the chance to use the airport's baggage scales for her weight records while the leaders struggled on with the baggage problems.

When eventually we got on the Twin Otter and had strapped ourselves in, an engine immediately developed problems and so we all got off again.

'Have you got a colour on your hair, Mags?' Susie asked me lazily, face cupped in her hands, staring glazily at my head as we sat idling the time away on a set of aircraft steps. We were watching the engineers probing the engine with a screwdriver. Up on a wall a group of monkeys sat inspecting each other. The engineers peered inside the engine with a torch, muttering; the monkeys peered inside each other's ears, jabbering.

'Yes, a henna rinse,' I replied, 'to protect it from the sun.'

'I thought so' she said, sounding thoroughly bored.

'Well, it'll be like straw by the time we get back,' I said. 'If you remember, the sun, on the Baltoro.'

'Oh yes,' she said dreamily. 'Could be grey before we get away from here.'

Little did we realize how wrong we were about the sun!

An hour and a half later we were back on board and Joy, nervously swigging whisky from her hip flask, generously offered it around. She had turned a pale shade of green and was frightened of the flight, probably shrewdly so, if not prophetically. An hour later, well into the mountains and in dense cloud cover, the pilot announced that he couldn't find the landing field at Tumlingtar. Joy grabbed her bottle.

'Don't worry, Joy, he looks quite old,' Nigel said, 'so he must be good or he wouldn't be here himself.'

She clung on to her flask and we all stiffened a little. The pilot announced we were going back.

The steward laughed when we thanked her for the nice ride – as we'd circled Kathmandu a few times, giving us a wonderful bird's eye view of the city which lies in a lush valley at four thousand feet. There are two other towns: Patan, which is adjacent to Kathmandu, and Braktaphur, a few miles away. The valley was surrounded by snow-capped mountains, and tier upon tier of luminous green paddy fields – dissected by the two rivers, the Bagmati and the Manaharathe – stretched out from the towns and coated every inch of the hilly valley. They have a two-crop season, spring wheat and autumn rice, both of which are renowned for their colour. Sometimes the tiers are yellow with flowering mustard or pink with apple blossom. The great *stupa* – the largest in the country – stood out clearly in its circular setting and the King's palace, although not huge, was edged by lovely gardens. Kathmandu is a wonderfully exciting city, with an exotic mix of race, religion and culture. Nepal is primarily Hindu but the mountain people are Buddhists with a strong Tibetan influence. Both these, and other minor religious groups, coexist in complete harmony. The ancient Indian-inspired, and 1930s 'English' architecture, is combined with many fine examples of the half-finished derelict style and certain parts of the city, like Patan, are linked together by a maze of mysterious, eastern alleyways. Markets, temples and shops abound, and a great deal of life is lived in the street, along with the animals. The holy cows, for instance, all belong to an owner and, while they roam the city at will all day, they find their way home at night in time for milking. Delhi is unkindly called 'smelly Delhi', but Kathmandu is culture-shock personified and we call it Krazy Kathmandu because it is so stimulating. When, in the early part of this century, King Birendra Bir Bikram Shah Dev's father wanted motor cars in the country, they were carried on poles by his subjects from India through the mountains and then floated across the river. The King's edict that tourists should 'take nothing but pictures, leave nothing but footprints and kill nothing but time' seemed to epitomize the gentle wisdom of Nepal's ancient culture – especially after Dr Kamal Kumar Shrestha observed that 'tourism is not only the goose that lays the golden egg but it also fouls it own nest', a sad but accurate indictment of it. King Birendra decreed Nepal a 'Zone of Peace' and announced that it would be 'sunny and dry throughout the kingdom from October to March'. A lovely Camelot ideal – but what about August and September?

During the evening meal, back in the Narayani Hotel, Joan taught us Midlanders a few applicable Northern words like 'clarty' (thick and muddy) and 'fl-a-t-us' (flatulence) while Andy and Simon told jokes of every hue as we speculated about the dreaded leech, likely to be evident in monsoon time where we were going. They seemed to be something people spoke about with a hooded caution and a degree of repugnance. As a result of the excitement and nervousness, we didn't sleep a wink that night. We'd left all the bags at the airport (to save clearing them again the next day) and now we found that though we slept in only a dash of perfume, the heat, the unfamiliar, incessant squeak of crickets, the throaty snapping and snarling of dogs outside our window – and the rumbling of tummies with fl-a-t-us – were no friends of rest.

By three o'clock Susie was sick. At half-past four, the croaking telephone rang (with our morning call) and she was sick again. At breakfast they served bacon and eggs and the smell had the same devasting effect. The bus ride to the airport didn't help her either, though, unfortunately in the urgency of the moment, she was unable to miss a man's bicycle which was leaning against the wall. He rushed over and snatched it away, rather crossly.

Only a few clouds marred the view from the plane on this, our second day, and we came clearly on to the landing field without any problems. Small children greeted us and scampered round the single-storey, single-roomed terminal. Through the fence, on which perched brilliantly coloured parrots, we could see our tents. The heat was intense, and wet clouds swirled up from densely forested hillsides in a thick mist. The air was opaque with bi-winged dragonflies. It looked and felt and sounded just like Burma – the Burma of the movies.

A meal was planned for eleven o'clock and then we would set off to Khandbari, but Susie was still sick and many of us had diarrhoea, so we weren't very hungry. This was all part of travelling in new countries and we accepted it, and mostly just ignored it, hoping we would soon adjust.

The intention was to walk a half day today, leaving at about one o'clock when Doug arrived, but as the time went on and he was obviously delayed, we pressed for moving on.

Because it was wet underfoot and looked a little like rain, we prepared our gaiters, but in fact it was so hot that we had to steel ourselves to put them on. We seemed to have lost our inertia – probably because we were feeling a bit weak. Nevertheless, we got to Khandbari, only one thousand feet up on nice paths, in good time and with only a minor incident when a couple of the group felt grotty from the unaccustomed heat.

During the night, long after we had gone to sleep, an eerie sound woke us. It was a band of villagers dancing and singing, but the unfamiliar sound of the instruments gave it a weird, sinister, occult ring to our ears. By 3.30, torrential rain also held our attention. The bed-*chi* came at half-past six, and by nine we'd left, in clarty mist.

We hadn't gained any height flying up to Tumlingtar, as it is 2,600 feet lower than Kathmandu, and the previous day's walk to Khandbari had brought us up to 3,800 feet. We were going up to 6,000 feet. The full group, fourteen trekkers, Andy (trek leader) and sixteen climbers, was together now. Doug, his daughter Martha,

Greg and Sharu had got into Tumlingtar late the previous night and camped farther down. They were coming up that morning.

We started off across acres of terraces, meticulously planted with rice and all knitted together with beans vines. We slotted through hamlets of straw-roofed houses dwarfed by waving maize. The maize husks were fed to the animals and the kernels ground, mostly by hand, with a stone mortar and pestle, for flour. We were astounded at the abundance of produce: rice, potatoes, a kind of kale, tiny cucumbers, onions, tomatoes (a few), limes, bananas (small, but thicker than ours), potatoes for the *chhang* (beer) and millet to make *tomba* or *rakshi* which, when it's fermented, is extremely alcoholic. Water buffaloes pulled the plough, tiny goats and cows provided the milk and cheese, small boars the meat, and the sheep provided wool. There were even plenty of cats, no doubt for the plenty of mice! Bougainvillaea, poinsettia, begonias, zinnias, and ferns grew in among the maize and added spots of lovely colour. Shading the homes were giant Jack fruit trees with leaves as big as dinner plates and this was indeed what the locals made with them. They shredded the leaves into strips and wove them into a plate. They even made pixie-like hats with them. Gliding through the air were kites and crows, cawing loudly, and egrets sat patiently on the bony backs of the cattle.

Sometimes, as we passed the houses, a father would rush out with a toddler in his arms and ask for medical help. They believed all Westerners were doctors, or that at least they would possess a panacea for their ills, and it always disturbed us when we couldn't help. All day the weather alternated between rain and fierce sunshine, and so we changed into our shorts but left on our boots and gaiters. The boots were for the rocky terrain, the gaiters for the leeches. We started to get quite blasé about the 'mythical leeches', of which we hadn't seen any so far, and we even began to believe that they weren't going to be a problem. A lot of tall stories, we thought, grossly exaggerated, and all those hunted, exchanged glances were just designed to unnerve us. We thought thus until we met the Frenchman. He was en route from Makalu to Tumlingtar and his legs were pitted with bites and suppurating sores, clotted and dripping with blood. 'Leeches,' he said when we asked what had happened – and we stopped joking immediately.

He told us that the weather had been extremely bad at BC, and that he hadn't been able to get across the river before base camp, because the bridge was down. That brought me up sharp. He had only once caught a fleeting glimpse of Makalu itself as it had been in cloud cover all the time, and another person, he warned, had been there for six days and hadn't seen it at all. That brought the lads up sharp.

It was a steep climb all day but an excellent lunch of delicious baby potatoes, cucumber and *pirranni* had knocked our psyche into a good walking frame and we three women plodded slowly on in a line, like Compo, Foggy and Clegg from 'Last of the Summer Wine'. The paths were narrow and led through a light foliage for the last three hours and we were in a carefree mood.

We saw John coming towards us. 'Look,' he said with an air of subterfuge, 'don't worry about it – but . . . '

'What?' we interrupted him.

'Well, it's a bit leechy.'

Just as if he had conjured one up in his hand, we suddenly saw the first one – on Susie's leg.

'Ugh,' she shuddered, slapping at it and trying to get it off. John pushed her had away and shouted, 'Don't touch it – I'll get it.' He grabbed a lighter from his pocket and burnt it off.

In the camp we found the gang gathered in a tight group, inspecting their arms and legs and checking their clothing. They were alternately laughing nervously or trying to be dismissive about it – our initiation to leeches.

Since the girls were arranging the tent, we had a nice big one this time, I went to the mess tent to write my diary, by the light of the kerosene lamps, and await dinner which, after three excellent meals already, we'd come to realize would be as different from the K2 diet of dal and rice as a broad brush-stroke is to pointillism. We were therefore looking forward to it. It was dark and I could hear the cook-boys chatting and cooking – and coughing – by the fire.

The dinner was a nightmare. The leeches saw to that. They turned it into a sort of St Vitus's Dance of Search by Torchlight as they crawled up our legs, down our collars, on our faces and over our hands. We panicked and the jovial bravado died in the shadows as we inspected each other's legs, bodies and heads. The food, which was terrific, suddenly became irrelevant.

Susie then finished us all off by telling us that a doctor had warned her of the leeches and told her to be careful when she went to the loo.

'Who?' we demanded to know.

'Us women – females,' she stressed, smirking a bit.

'That's right,' confirmed Joan, 'you must be very careful!'

Helen and I just looked at each other, aghast.

We girls had spent some pennies in some strange places and in unmentionable conditions, but this leech business introduced another, unwelcome, slant to the problem. So now we had to go with each other, and we created a scene like an anti-aircraft battery: torch beams criss-crossing as we scanned each other, one from the front, one from behind, checking the legs and trousers. We shook our heads in disbelief. Was there no end to the indignities we would put ourselves through just to see a mountain?

Walking-wounded tape comes in for many things, though rarely for its intended purpose, and rarely as a barricade. But we used it extensively to tape up the tent zip and pole holes before we could even contemplate settling down, and it was three very uneasy women who finally fell asleep that night.

2

Leech Alert and Earthquake

GLAD of the daylight, a leech-free night and porters who would 'do tents', we set off about nine o'clock.

This was the beginning of the rain forests, at six thousand feet. As we started out, it was grassy and shrubby, but we soon came into thickly wooded hillsides and entered an exotic cavern of ancient forests, an eerie world where no light shone through the dense canopy, and where the air was filled with strange, shrill bird calls and shrieking crickets. The living trees, only partially rooted in the soil, clawed desperately on to any rock surface with twisted, knotted roots. The ground was strewn with stumps, and fallen trees lay rotting in oozy black bogs. They were strangled and contorted and covered in lichens which crawled with insects. A grey-green vine, hanging like a fringe, coiled through everything, crossed the open spaces, and made a cobweb-like veil which brushed across your face every now and again. The air was heavy with moisture and it dripped continuously, adding to all the other weird sounds in a strange world.

We kept up a good pace, sometimes through the forests, sometimes through patches of open meadow-like areas with rocky outcrops thrusting up through the ground, because it was cold. We stopped only for thorough leech checks in our boots, gaiters and at our necks, following the path till we found ourselves high up on a ridge. To our right we looked back down the valley to Tumlingtar, in cloud, and on the left to dark mountains in mist and a cold, steel-grey lake. Later, beside an algae-covered pool, we met some of the group and discovered that the camp, in a small clearing called Murre, was just around the corner, on the top of the ridge.

'So soon,' we said, 'it's only been three hours!'

The porters wanted to camp here since the next camp – with water – was probably four more hours away. At this point, the sun was shining and we were delighted to settle down for a lazy afternoon.

As we lay on the grass, unthinkingly enjoying the pale sunshine, we noticed that Reg's shirt and trousers were covered in blood and asked him about it. He'd found that when he undid his trousers a leech had crawled inside his shirt and settled on his stomach. By the time he noticed it, it was already huge and bloated with blood and, when he had got it off, it had stained his clothes.

Then it started to rain, violently. After a wet lunch under brollies, and in a break from the downpour, we watched Martha with fascination. She searched out the leeches, which were all over the grass, and put them on her arm before casually salting them off with the *sang froid* of a fifteen-year-old – although there was nothing 'teen-aged' about Martha. She was a mature, well-read intellectual with a formidable knowledge of Nepal. She had first walked to Makalu base camp with her father and mother when she was nine years old; even her sister, who was only three, had gone with them. This was her third trip to Makalu and she approached it, not with our kind of apprehension or any need of our female company, but with an enviable confidence, putting us all to shame. We watched her handling the leeches in awe. 'They love the moist conditions between 4–10,000 feet,' she said, 'and the walk to Makalu is a favourite haunt!'

A leech is like a thin black worm, and it is everywhere, as it's spore is in the water – in the trees, the plants, the grass, the puddles. They normally live off the blood of animals, and vary in length from half an inch to two inches, with suckers at both ends of their bodies. With the back end suckered, they rear up their barely discernible heat-seeking heads in search of blood. If you put them on to a cold part of your hand, they will move, quite rapidly, flipping themselves over in a pincer-type movement towards the heat of a warm vein (say on your wrist), and then bite (not painfully) through to the blood and inject an anti-coagulant. When they are many times their own size, fat, bloated, satiated and quite disgusting, with several day's feed, they drop off. It's important not to pull them off, as that can cause infection. The best method of dealing with them is to make them withdraw by putting salt on them, or fire them with a lighter or a cigarette, all of which seem equally unpleasant acts, but are absolutely necessary. The horror tales of leeches are legion, such as the one about someone falling asleep with his mouth open and having a leech crawl in his throat. When it was bloated, it nearly choked him to death, or that one should be careful about washing water as the spores may get inside one's nose, etc, and they can live, for some time, off the blood inside. One was always being told, or warned, that they can slime through the most microscopic of openings, even bootlace eyelets, so we were well covered and hoped not to encounter these sort of problems.

But the rain didn't leave us for long and down it came again, fiercely, soaking us through as we helped the porters get the tents up.

Inside our tent we girls grabbed some dry clothes and I dragged off my damp shirt. There was a sudden numbed silence, unusual with us three girls, and Susie said quietly, 'Hang on a minute, Mags,' and the tension in her voice warned me that something was terribly wrong.

I swung round. 'Why – what is it?' I called out, scanning about for whatever it was. And suddenly I felt something on the inside of my arm, and looking down, I saw it – a huge, hideous, slimy, black, fully bloated, loathsome, vile leech – on my left breast. 'Ugh! No!' I cried in disgust.

'Oh God, Sue,' Helen called out, 'that's another one!'

'What the hell do you mean?' I demanded.

'There's two on your back!' she said quietly.

I slumped in despair. 'Oh God – I can't bear this – get them off me!' I pleaded.

We fought to remain calm. I don't know now whether they removed them with salt or the lighter, I couldn't see and I didn't care and I couldn't cope. They worked urgently, without speaking. When the job was done I sat, feeling quite sick, with my shirt off – to wait for the blood to stop flowing. We timed it: it was forty-five minutes before it clotted. We were all subdued with nausea and loathing and I was freezing cold. Out came the whisky.

As we questioned how this had happened, we realized that, because they are full of the host's blood and therefore the same body temperature as the host, it is impossible to feel them. They must have slithered inside my shirt as we sat on the grass earlier – now we could see how Reg hadn't felt his – and we stopped laughing at Susie's warning. Leech Alert was on.

Andy came to check his trekkers, as he often did, and as the whisky (only a few swigs) had buoyed us up, and we were more relaxed, we told him about the leeches. He, kindly, returned later with a small donation to our 'medicinal' supplies. 'Just in case,' he

said with a nod and a wink and, thanking him, we stowed it away
– for a rainy day!

'I wish I had a set of your Thomas Telfords now, Helen,' I said.
'I could do with a bit of extra protection.'

'Do with what?' Susie asked pointedly.

'Helen's Thomas Telfords,' I said, nodding at Helen's bra.

'Why do you call them Thomas Telfords?' she queried, wrinkling
her brow.

'You've seen the wire construction in them, haven't you?'

'What do you mean.'

'Well, I reckon there's more support wire in Helen's bra than on
the Forth Bridge. Thomas Telford? – Forth Bridge? He'd have been
proud of these,' and because I could see Susie frowning with confusion, I kidded her again. 'She's got a winch on them,' I said.

Susie started to grin and looked at Helen, who sat at the back of
the tent laughing silently like Muttly and not really taking any
notice. 'Don't be so awful.'

'It's true – look at them, they can stand up on their own – they've
got that much wire in them.'

'Oh, stop it,' she said and picked up Helen's bra. She looked at
it for a moment, and then suddenly tossed it away in hysterics and
fell on her back laughing. I see what you mean, that ought to keep
the leeches out – I should think they'd keep anything out.'

We all roared with laughter, and as I watched their faces, so
changed from their earlier expressions, I wondered where we would
be without our humour, childish though it is sometimes. That was
our oxygen – our lifeline!

The repeat, evening performance of the St Vitus's Dinner Dance
took on a new dimension. This time it had bloodstained costumes,
explicit dialogue, and a single thrust to the narrative: leech infes-
tation. Bryan's shirt was positively covered in blood and no matter
how diligently we searched they still appeared all over us – but not,
as yet, in the *nearly* most dreaded place of all: the hair. Noticeably,
neither male nor female differed in their panic about the repulsive
leech and, just to compound the problem, not one of us had escaped
the bowel disorder either – despite the excellent food.

Back in the tent after an intensive clothing and boot inspection,
Helen announced that she had to make a visit. Now 'even a king
has to go on his own – to sit on the throne' and we had two
throneless holes in ground, and the Poire Belle was called to attend.
This was not a visit to be relished, but when the call comes one is

left with no choice and she, unenviably, crawled out into the rain, gaitered, waterproofed, brollied, torchlit and purse-lipped. Of course as soon as she was off the premises, Susie and I battened down the hatches, shutting her out and repelling all boarders, while we rolled out the sleeping bags and began to scrutinize them exhaustively.

Five minutes later we heard a running, calling, crying Helen. When she reached the tent and clawed at the opening, she was screaming, 'Quick, open the tent – Mags, Sue – open the tent! Hurry – hurry – come on – come on, open it up.'

We scrambled to unzip the flap, alarmed by her frenzy.

'What is it – what's the matter?'

She tried to get in.

'No, don't get in – we haven't checked you for leeches – wait – wait!'

'Oh, I can't – I can't,' she screeched, 'let me in,' and she just fell inside.

We looked despondently at her. She was covered in water and what we strongly suspected was leech-infested mud.

'What's the matter – what happened?'

'Leeches in the loo – the tent – it's full of them – everywhere all over the ground – on the sides – over your head – a nightmare!'

We froze. The hair!

'Oh God, it's so awful I couldn't stand it – I felt hysterical I couldn't get my trousers up – I had to just hold on to them as I ran through the pouring rain. John heard me and called after me – but I couldn't wait – I even left my brolly there – I was so terrified.' She paused for breath.

Susie and I fell silent for a second. She caught my eye and I bit my lip; I knew what was coming. We daren't look at Helen, so forlorn under her dripping hood and clothing awry, and her eyes widened, appalled, as she began to realize that we were trying to stifle the laughter. We couldn't help it. Once Susie let out the first suppressed snort, and her shoulders began to shake, we all got the hysterics.

'Good job you had the Thomas Telfords on then,' I spluttered, as we wondered where it would all end.

'For God's sake let's get ourselves sorted out,' Susie said when we'd recovered. 'We'd better start with Helen's boots – ready with the torches everyone – look together. If there's even the smallest one in here, I'll be up all night scanning the tent with the torch.'

We taped the tent up obsessively and the wind started to blow. When we finally lay, anxiety-ridden, in our sleeping bags, the wind beat so fiercely on the canvas that I couldn't hear what Helen and Susie were saying to each other – even though they were lying next to me. I thought it was because we were up on top of the ridge, that the winds from both sides met head-on, making fierce squalls. But, with the rain beating down and the wind howling, it was so tempestuous that we decided to take sleeping tablets so that we could sleep, and eventually, exhausted by our little traumas, we fell into a disturbed sleep.

At first I thought the big, rocking movement I could feel was Susie scrambling out of her sleeping bag to get away from leeches. Then I realized it was more than that – and sat bolt-upright. It was pitch dark – and all the alarm bells of hell were ringing. The tent was rolling in a wide arc from side to side and the ground heaved up and shuddered violently beneath us.

'What is it?' Susie called out in terror – but Helen and I were so frozen with cold fear that we couldn't answer. 'God – it's an earthquake,' she breathed in terror. 'The whole mountain is moving. Oh my God.'

'Quick – get your boots on,' I shrieked. Panic set in and we tore at the confining zips of our sleeping bags, trying to get free.

The ground rumbled on and the tent rocked maniacally. Suddenly I was convinced we were going to slip down the mountainside with a great slice of mountain, to be buried alive in the small pocket of air that the tent would make – and then it stopped. For a moment, there was a terrible, paralysing silence, loaded with uncertainty. We waited, taut with fear, dreading it starting again, holding on to the floor as if to stop it moving, wondering what was going to happen next. Silence, then slowly people started to call out to each other, checking who was still there – 'You OK, girls?' John called. We called back, in trembling voices. Then Nigel released the safety valve with a light-hearted 'Nigelism': 'Don't worry girls, it's only an earthquake – a tent's the best thing to be in.'

It was hard to assimilate this quip, at that moment, but it sounded comforting – and we relaxed a little. The ground might have stopped shaking, but we didn't, for some time. It might have lasted only a few seconds on a Richter scale somewhere, but it was a lifetime on our Fearometer. We didn't sleep again, just sat rigid in our beds, and remarked on the fact that in the last twenty-four hours, we'd had twelve hours of torrential rain, gales, leeches in awful places and earthquakes – and now it was five o'clock in the morning, we were shattered – and had to get up and go on.

3

Monsoons, Mudslides and Mashed *Rakshi*

Two days after the earthquake we'd been through Num and Seduwa. Seen under a canvas of sunlight, they would be lovely Nepalese villages. We saw them painted in mist, heavy rain and mud, and we were ourselves driven by the mawl-stick of sickness and low morale.

We dropped all the way down from Num, at 5,000 feet, to the wide, rushing river Arun at 2,400 feet, it being the only route through. The rocky paths, flowing with water, cut through jungly undergrowth which was pierced by junipers, pines and holly oaks. Here again everything was cobwebbed in hanging vines, and the warning howls of a family of monkeys competed with the frenzied crescendo of crickets. We came to the bridge, and the porters placed a flower talisman in their hair for the crossing and indicated we do the same, and I thought I was going to be able to negotiate it quite well as it was new, and solid, with sides, but the fear and trembling were still there! Then we were back up to 5,000 feet again at Seduwa, all in thick misty rain.

Both days, when we arrived in the wet, we found Nigel taking beer, or *rakshi*, in a tea house while the tents went up. And because the houses contained leech-eating chickens, and were therefore relatively horror-free, we all squeezed in the tiny rooms and drank the mashed *rakshi* (rice wine). It was milky and gritty and cost five rupees a glass. The Indian beer was twelve, but it was a welcome, warming drink at the end of the day and helped dry us out and balance the scales of discomfort. In Seduwa, the landlady offered her ten-year-old daughter in marriage to Simon as she romped all over him in childlike play. Needless to say Simon, even through a *rakshi* haze, was somewhat nonplussed.

John had two problems. One was that he had a new tent, which he had bought for his own use, and it leaked. The other was a severe attack of foot rot, from wet socks and boots, which would lead to painful blistering if he were not careful. Bathing them in salt water helped.

I missed the evening meal, having got dreadful stomach cramps, as most of us had, and spent it prostrate in the tent, listening to the porters singing. They probably drank the *rakshi* as well, and they certainly deserved it after their hard days of carrying. It is lovely to be back with Nepalese porters again, since they reminded us of Pemba. They were so much brighter and sunnier than the brusque Baltistanis, and they definitely sang more along the trail. In particular, it would be the bare-foot *sherpanis* who seemed to lead the song, and the others would join in the chorus, cheering us all along. I expect they talked about the earthquake, as Dorjee (our head *sirdar*) had told us that he and the some of the porters had clung on to the tent pole throughout the movement and said a lot of prayers.

One of the *sirdars* heard on his radio that the earthquake was quite serious and that a lot of people had died in India, along with three hundred in Nepal. It was forty seconds long and rated 6.7 on the Richter scale. We wondered if the news of it would reach England to worry our families and asked Doug if we could send news back. He said that a runner had gone down to Tumlingtar and that a message would get through to Kathmandu and then to England.

We didn't think there were as many leeches at Seduwa, and we were relieved about that, as the diarrhoea, the rain and the wind were plenty to cope with and now we were perturbed about another problem: our wet clothes. We didn't relish the thought that the next day we would have to put on wet clothes. The following morning, however, Joan woke with a leech on her lip. They were there just the same.

The sky was clear and blueish and although it might get hot around midday, we still expected to see rain later, as that seemed to be the pattern of the weather, raining most of the afternoon. Helen had slept badly and Susie, normally so reliable and stout-hearted, despaired. Tearfully, she announced that she wanted to go home, to get out of this wet. With my arm around her, I reminded her of how she had said that at K2, and her courage, which I knew was only just below the surface, reasserted itself.

As coping with wet, smelly clothes started to pall, and the reasons for being here remained as elusive as ever, I began to understand just how much fortitude it did take to go on. It was not always easy to find the motivation. There had also been a small fracas between trekkers and trek leaders at dinner the previous night, Nigel being both spokesman and outspoken, about going on the following day. I missed it, being in my tent, but Susie was hoping for the, talked about, rest and recovery period, and I concluded that the absence of this was the reason for her low spirits. But she had a great capacity for suffering and willed herself on. It takes bitter-sweet ingredients to make a rich cake, I know, but so far we were still only grating the lemon.

We were heading for Tashigoan at 7,000 feet, making steep climbs. Generally the day's walking wasn't hard, a steady five hours in drier weather, but the mist never left us, and the clouds swirled around the tops of the trees, leaving us with a very limited view. The hillsides around us were still thickly covered in forestation, sometimes scarred by burnt areas, and our path skirted the thick woods and wove through cultivated terraces. Houses and tiny villages clung to the hillsides for miles around, blessed by an abundance of water from endless waterfalls which ran down into the paddy fields and irrigation ditches.

We bought bananas from one village, at a rupee for two, and the sky, suddenly clearing, gave us a dry and lazy lunch. There was plenty of interchange with the climbers over the meal— which was nice. They came from all walks of life, and varied in their approach to the seriousness of their climb. For some, just enjoying the climb as far as they could go was their objective, whereas Doug intended to take the west face along with Sharu, Simon Yates, Greg Childs, Mark Millar and Rick Allen. Taking the couloir route was Andy Parkin (a painter), Praful Mistry, Alan Hinkes, Dr Brian McCowan, Dr Kirsten Box and Terry Mooney. Martha, Laurent Parkin (Andy's wife) and Allison (Rick's wife) were taking things as they came – I believed. Terry, an old buddy of Doug's, was emerging as an interesting Irishman with deep convictions about his work as a QC (the youngest, at forty-nine, in Belfast) – he defended IRA terrorists. It seemed he had a real motive for coming to the Himalayas, as a four-month break, and a life-threatening climb, would certainly divert his mind from the stressful career of dealing with other people's traumas. He spent most of the time telling stories and jokes with typical lyrical Irish flair and sometimes found solace in an ample supply of hooch. He also had the knack of reviving Susie's sense of humour, as when he replied to her inquiry as to how he was feeling by saying, 'A bit tight-cheeked.' She chuckled over that for hours.

We started to fall into a pattern of walking with the same people.

This was inevitable, and usually due to the speed one walked and how one related to others. Nigel, Andy and Simon raced ahead with Joy (a very strong walker) with Peter, Reg and Steve close behind. I walked with Peter, the civil engineer, who told us stories of the sewerage system in London, and the young Bryan from Brighton. John, Susie and Helen walked together and Joan, who loved to walk with the porters and generally did so, moved from one group to another, spreading her considerable humourous largesse. Sometimes we even walked with the climbers, and when I walked with Alan Hinckes he asked me, 'How can you tell the difference between a trekker and a climber?'

'By their sanity,' I hazarded.

'No – because trekkers have fallen for all the sales hype and bought all the gear – climbers only buy carrying gear.' He was right about that, as they seemed to wear not much more than skimpy shorts, T-shirts and colourful bandanas – but carried immense, professional-looking backpacks. 'And they don't wear designer outdoor gear, or bring umbrellas!'

Well, I said that since John and I had got only pink pack-a-macs we could hardly be accused of emulating the designer climber clothes set and put the case of the brolly versus the ski pole to him. Granted, it wasn't much of a shield in the 'real' rain, I said, but at least you could use it as a walking stick – and as a screen for the women in embarrassing moments, unlike a ski-pole. A valid point, I thought, till he asked me: 'Then why does John carry one?'

There wasn't any answer to that, I said, and he said, 'It isn't the kind of problem men generally bother about.'

'Ah yes, but John does think about us all the time – that's why we bring him along you know!' And we laughed.

Tashigoan was a handful of houses surrounding a great big, lovely, hand-made, timber and stone building – all of thirty feet long – the village hall-cum-school. The early birds had established themselves in the loft, and when we arrived they were sitting out of the rain under the huge eaves in the open doorway of the corn shute, jeering at us last damp stragglers-in.

Presumably a small recompense for the hire of the hall was negotiated, and twenty or more rolled out their carry mats, hung up their wet clothes and looked pretty cosy in there. The roof leaked only a little bit. But as we girls established our six-by-three space, late in the afternoon, up came the smoke through the floorboards from the cooking fire below and nearly asphyxiated Susie and out came the vapours from Helen when Andy Watts discovered a full-blown leech in her hair. Horror of all horrors! So, with Helen in a state of shock, we scuttled out of the building and into the tents, thinking we could patrol a small space more easily. Susie and Helen shared a tent and I took over a spare one. Before settling, we braved the elements and mingled among the camp activities.

Dorjee was paying off the porters, fifty rupees for thirty kilos and one hundred rupees for sixty. Reading from his well-used exercise book, he ticked off the names and payments due. In most cases the porters couldn't sign their names, so they pressed their thumbs on a small ink pad and made their print in the book, marking it with a cross. Dorjee, as witness, left his first fingerprint and signed that.

A couple of other porters, kneeling on a tarpaulin with a sharp knife wedged crossways between their knees, cut up, with infinite attention to detail, a beast – probably a water buffalo. They had numerous little piles of meat, each on a small sheet of polythene, on to which was placed a slice or handful of every part of the carcass – offal, lights, liver, muscle, bone. Each pile had no more nor less than the others. The porters paid for this meat with their wages and even the village people bought some. Sometimes a beast was killed and hung up to smoke in the houses, Dorjee told us. He said that he 'no like flesh'; unlike the dogs, who snapped, snarled and drew blood as the men tossed them scraps to keep them away. It was cheering to see plenty of chickens strutting around, and we hoped they were busy eating leeches.

Just as I was rolling off a 400 ASA (the fastest film I had), trying to capture the clarty surrounding and the loo tent going up in a moor-like mist, Doug strolled in. He was feeling unwell and immediately went to bed in the loft. He'd been struggling with a debilitating attack of diarrhoea and was taking homoeopathic medicines, melissa and the like. We took Lomatil, a powerful chemical medicine, which helped a little, some of the time.

The rain started in earnest about five o'clock in the evening. We squelched along to the mess tent and, sitting under brollies inside it, ate an excellent dinner, getting up only occasionally, between leech searches, to prod the pools of water off the roof with our brollies, before it brought the tent down. Umtu, a new Pemba, and Bhom were our cooks. They did a super job, so cheerfully, and laughed at our fear of the leeches with their triffid-like antennae up searching for blood. But the leeches were everywhere and we kept a constant, nerve-racking watch – and had stopped laughing about them altogether. A beautiful, huge cricket was trapped in the tent and it came and sat on one of the mugs, attracted to the warmth and light of the spluttering candles. We attempted, with all the torches beamed on it, to get a photograph; 'like they have in the *National Geographic*', someone said, because that was how it looked.

Whether it was the tensions caused by the leeches or the extraordinary rain, which was louder than my Walkman, or the news of four thousand feet tomorrow, or the jazzy Indian music, or the lentil soup, or the several massive cracking sounds in the ground or just being in the tent on my own for the first time, or even the wet socks drying out in my sleeping bag, I don't know – but all the demons of the night seemed to visit me, and I spent a demented, tortured night. At 5.30 I dragged myself out of bed and listened to the rain.

The girls had suffered a sleepless night themselves, they told me at 5.50 in the morning; they'd been half expecting another earthquake. John was fine in the building – but after twelve hours of rain I felt depression set in. I wrote two words in my diary that morning: survival and lunacy, and then these four lines

> At Makalu I'm learning a thing or two – new,
> Though some things never alter.
> The fears are the same as we felt at K2,
> But this rain – may make us falter.

My wet trousers stuck coldly to my legs. I struggled miserably to pull them on. The grubby, damp, smelly T-shirt stuck to my head and wouldn't slide on. I dragged at it in the cold and saw how the hideous, inelegant Tubyfoam I put round my toes to prevent blisters had turned black with the mud, and could have cried. I crawled out into the torrential rain, worried about how we were going to get through the day.

4

Faltering

I T was 7.30 in the evening of day eight in the tent at Kauma. Kauma by name – trauma by nature. Shivering with cold, I sat in a peculiar kind of bemused amazement – and utter disbelief. The rain was thundering on the tent in its thirtieth hour without a break. We expected it to rain all night, just as it had done for the previous two and wondered what happened to the brief afternoon spells of rain.

John and I, now sharing a tent, were sitting huddled in our pile jackets, tucked into our sleeping bags and trying to keep warm. I should have been looking for my balaclava in my kitbag – but I was afraid it would be like the rest of our things – wet.

We were all in a state of shock about this monsoon; it was abnormally heavy. Normally it would rain for one or two hours at a stretch – then clear and, during the nine trips Doug has made to Makalu, he had never experienced the like of this one. We had obviously been unlucky to walk into these extreme conditions, though it was probably running true to form, worldwide, as weather patterns do seem, in the last few years, to have become more extreme.

We had walked six hours on this particular day, five of them in relentless rain, coming up 3,500 feet, climbing vertically some of the time – straight up stream beds. It had been water, water and more water, with the temperature dropping rapidly which made the conditions absolutely horrendous. This time it wasn't the rapid ascent to 11,600 feet that fazed us, though that was very hard; it was the rain and the cold – and the touch of hypothermia at the end of it.

Somehow we had got way ahead of the porters, and arrived at the camp long before them – and of course before the tents. Unfortunately, while we waited in the wind, rain and cold, Helen, who was particularly susceptible to this problem, began to suffer badly. We crowded around her, wrapped her in a carry mat and tried to keep her warm. As soon as the tent was up, we got her in it, blue with cold. She was in difficulties – and so Greg and Mark produced some semi-dry sleeping bags and a survival blanket. In an hour or so she'd recovered. There were seven of us in all in that tent trying to get dry, and between us we managed to make Greg's and Mark's clothing and bedding even more wet and muddy than they already were. But they didn't mind, and everyone cheered up quite quickly. Meanwhile John, Doug (still sick), Andy and the porters struggled to erect the rest of the tents in the pouring rain and sloshing mud.

Eventually they got Susie and Helen into their own tent, and four hours after arriving at the camp site John finally got into the tent we were now sharing – soaked through to the bone, freezing and very concerned. Our clothes, boots and carry mats were so wet that we just left them outside in the rain, lying in pools of water. How to cope with this sort of wet, and with our wet clothes, was becoming a serious problem. Even the insides of our rucksacks were saturated – not to mention smelly. We did have polythene bags (dustbin liners), inside polythene bags, inside rucksacks and, at the moment, they were standing up to it reasonably well, keeping the odd item dry – but I didn't think they would do so for much longer, as they were splitting all the time. 'I'll never come again without a really heavy waterproof liner in my rucksack, I thought.

Meanwhile, the porters, sherpas and sherpanis carried up thirty- and sixty-pound loads in T-shirts, shorts and flip-flops, some even in bare feet. They continued to run around the camp, helping to sort everyone out – and I had seen that the cook-boys were getting a meal. Sure enough, they brought the dinner around to all the tents later, and by then I was fully convinced that climbers do measure hardship by a yardstick different from the one employed by us mere mortals. I also knew why sherpas made such brilliant Gurkhas: they are peerless in their hardiness.

I could hear Joy and Joan hooting with laughter in their tent, and Nigel calling out to them. I wondered if it was a sort of reaction to the awfulness, as I knew they all had terrible stomach problems. Bryan's were the worst, but he didn't complain.

As John and I lay on the cold ground (the carry mats outside), enveloped by discomfort, he delivered the dreaded line, the one we'd been thinking about – but were avoiding. 'We should go down! It's a pointless exercise! We've got nothing to prove – and we should consider Helen.'

Though I knew it was coming, it was still a terrible bombshell, and somehow I didn't want to hear it – but we did have to think about Helen. Sensing my reluctance, he said, 'We'll talk to the girls in the morning. Look, we haven't got the right rain gear for this. We'd be crazy to go on in these conditions, and it will only get colder the farther up we get. The sooner we get out of it the better – it's ridiculous. We'll go to India.'

I didn't say anything, and sank into a deep despondency. I knew it was madness going on, but couldn't come to terms with going down – and more puzzling still, I didn't know why. Surely we *should* go down? Of course we should, but was this 'our John' suggesting that we back out? Our John of the great outdoors, of all the courage, the adventurous spirit, that inspired us all? If he was feeling negative – what of us? We weren't strong without John, and now we'd arrived at a hideous crossroads. We were forced to make a decision none of us wanted to make, but which way to turn, up or down?

First thing in the morning – and in the thirty-eighth hour of rain – John had gone to see the girls. He'd spent a bad night suffering with a headache and so had Helen. She also had a cold and, worse still, woke to find a leech on her face. Susie was nervous about Helen and John returned to tell me, 'That's it – we're going down!' I'll go and tell Doug, and arrange for a couple of porters to take our bags. Hang on to them, by the way. We don't want the porters to take them on.' He was shouting at me through the tent door, standing in driving rain and slipping about in the mud, shaking with the cold – and still, though I knew this was plumbing the depths, I didn't want to go down. But: 'one goes we all go', and so I began to pack my bags with a heavy heart, trying to accept the decision and resigning myself to giving up.

We four were first over to the mess tent for breakfast, not having to hurry with our packing, and the others drifted in through the Somme-like conditions, wearing their depression like a badge. When John announced that we weren't going on, and they'd stopped reeling from the shock and finally believed us, a great wave of melancholy washed over the whole group. Bonds do undeniably grow, unconsciously, and to break them in a time of need feels disloyal and weak; Joan started to think hard about coming back with us, though we had no intention of undermining others' resolve.

While we were still discussing it, Doug, Sharu and Martha walked in. 'Hang on a minute,' Doug said. 'Nobody's going anywhere. The porters have left.' The shock-wave returned, silencing everyone.

'Well, not all of them,' Doug said, 'but the Hille men and women – they have taken their things and gone. They don't feel they're equipped for these conditions, and I've arranged for them to send some more men back.' He smiled at John. 'Anyway, youth, perhaps it's just as well to stay here – for today at least.' Feeling bombarded with emotion and confusion, we stared at each other – not knowing what to think.

Terry, who by now had arrived in the mess tent, along with some of the other climbers, was standing beside me. We were looking across the table at a cold, cheerless Helen, and he said, 'I think I can see someone who could do with a bit of a cuddle, don't you'

I swung round to look at him, and saw in his eyes a welcome compassion. 'Oh, Terry – that's really kind – I'm sure she does.'

'I'll look after her for a while,' he continued. 'She'll be all right.' And with a twinkle in his Irish eyes, he squelched round the table, pulled up a stool beside her, tried unsuccessfully to level it in the mud, plopped down on the wobbly stool and put his arm around her. As he produced a half-bottle of 'medicament' from his poacher's pocket, sliding it on to the table, her questioning eyes shot round first to Terry's and then across the table to mine. Her face beamed with a perky smile. Some minutes later, when we heard her bell-like laugh ring out, Susie and I grinned knowingly at each other – and I felt a great weight lift off my shoulders. It was 7.30 a.m!

John was lying in his bed reading his book, his Walkman glued to the ears, his resolve to go down unmoved. It was early afternoon and after the games of cards, swigs of rum, the jokes about the Somme, and a good lunch, we'd put a more buoyant Helen to bed and were all keeping out of the rain.

I was lying in my sleeping bag and John was still reading when Doug unzipped the tent and fell in – cold and wet – and a fascinating conversation began. It started on the subject of the previous day's problems, when we over-anxious trekkers, afraid of taking too long to get to camp, had left much too soon and before the porters could get away (a lesson to us all), and touched on the practicalities of handling the trek in these conditions. Then it changed imperceptibly into the topic of 'the health of the mind', the predicament of the life force leaving the body and the regaining of the life force through spiritual energy. If we'd had that spiritual energy, we wouldn't have lost the nucleus of that essential life force – which we now needed to regain.

Only after a while did I realize that Doug was practising the subtlest form of persuasion, whether intended or not, and it was directed at John. 'Don't come all that bollocks with me, Scott. I don't know what you're talking about, anyway – life force and all that stuff – we're going down and that's that. The girls want to go!' he stated, waving his hand towards me to solicit confirmation.

I muttered quietly, 'Well, I'm not sure about that.'

He stopped. 'What do you mean?'

'The girls don't want to go down,' I said.

'Yes, of course they do – you probably don't – but Helen and Susie . . . '

'No, not Susie,' I said, 'and I don't think Helen wants to go down now either.'

'How do you know that?'

'Susie and I talked about it by the loo tent; we do all our best talking there, when it's not raining too much – and she said Helen was in such a good frame of mind after the rest and the food, and Terry's tipple and that . . . '

'Bugger me,' he expostulated and sank back. 'Well, I s'pose if that's what you' – and he swung round to Doug, who was smiling broadly 'you so and so, Scott – gotta give it to you though – you handled that pretty well. Oh well, I s'pose if the girls want to go on . . . but I'm buggered if I know why. So that's it. Have you got any decent rain gear we could borrow? – Mags and I haven't got anything for this blasted awful stuff.'

'That's no problem; I'll get you some later. You can have mine, and Mags can have Sharu's expedition gear.'

When Doug had left and John had finished huffing and puffing, I found myself smirking under the sleeping bag at Doug's astute reversal of John's decision – and at my own irrational pleasure at the thought of going on. But I still couldn't think of any sane reason *why*. The need for the risk, or arousal, factor in our lives must be very strong – or terribly undernourished, I thought, as I listened to the pelting rain.

Incredibly, that night, in this hideous blot on the landscape, the cook-boys produced an extraordinarily good meal. Doug decided it was important and Sharu supervised it. Without doubt it was a remarkable feat, and much appreciated by us all. Thirty-five of us crushed into our one mess tent (it was not worth the trouble of putting two up in the wind and rain), and with candles on the check tablecloth, we ate egg drop soup and croutons, rice, eggs, bean sauce, spaghetti, roast potatoes and some meat in sauce – followed by custard and pots of tea to finish. I was glad of that, as I was back on my gallons of tea a day for the altitude.

At one stage, out of curiosity and a need to remind myself of others' hardship, I went over to see how they had produced this amazing meal. It was being cooked in a Stygian hole of a kitchen, under a tarpaulin, and carried through the pouring rain, and swamp, by torchlight. And when it was all over, these terrific men, after dinner, would sleep in the mess tent among the wet kit, under the dripping roof, with only a blanket between them and the quagmire.

Terry, who had apparently continued his excellent therapy all afternoon, didn't make it to dinner – pity really, I thought, as somehow I felt I owed him a drink.

5

Shipton La

'WHAT's that?' I said, waking out of a deep slumber.
  'What?' John said.
'That? Silence? My God, it's not raining.'

It was ten past six and silent: no drumming on the tent, no blustering flapping wind, no dripping canvas running with water, just silence, beautiful silence.

'It hasn't been raining for the last hour,' John said, packing his bag, 'and about time as well.'

I agreed with him, and as I cast my eyes around the brighter light of the tent, said, 'That's sixty hours then, I reckon – sixty hours of continuous torrential rain. Do you think it's all over at last?' I waited, hoping he'd tell me he thought it was, but he just muttered a dubious, non-committal 'Hmm.'

At breakfast we discovered that we were going up 2,500 feet over Shipton La, one of the highest passes in the Himalayas, at 13,000 feet. Then we would drop down 1,200 feet. That was the bit we didn't like. Every thousand feet we dropped down had to be regained in the next day or so, which meant harder work at altitude, but one had to pass through the folds of the mountains where there was access. We were running a bit behind time at this point, because of the extraordinary weather conditions. This was the ninth day and we were meant to do it in ten. The problem would come at base camp: would there be enough time to go up to 21,000 feet? Our flights home kept us to this timetable, but monsoons are not respecters of airline schedules. Andy Norris kept us informed about the route every day and we traced the elevations on a small map that we had. There was a long day ahead!

Doug made sure the porters were away before us and while we were waiting for the last remaining few to leave we walked up the hill behind the camp. We looked back at Kauma, thinking of how unhappy we'd been there – and of how that tiny little churned-up mud patch, lost in miles of misty mountains, looking so innocuous, so inconsequential, had, along with the rain, nearly defeated us. We were happy to turn our backs on it.

Seven hours later, we arrived at Mumbuk, a camp set handsomely among tall pine trees and craggy cliffs. We had no eye for this beauty, however: our vision was completely distorted by a record day of horror. Relief was all we felt at the sight of the tents and I had only one word to describe the day in the diary: 'Purgatory!' It had rained from beginning to end. We had suffered headaches, nausea, breathlessness, exhaustion, mud, hours of walking through icy-cold streams and waterlogged grass; and all the while a raw, biting cold cut straight through us. We fell on the unstable rocks of the stream, not getting any wetter, and Susie twisted her knee. Because of the thick mist and low cloud we saw nothing over the Shipton La except the lakes as we waded through the boggy edges of them. Reg was hit by a falling rock (which luckily missed his head and hit his rucksack – though it damaged his camera), and another rock missed Andy's head by inches. There were moments of panic when Helen was trying to get over a rockslide, and Joan was convinced that she had cerebral oedema. Our boots, full of water, squelched us up, two and a half thousand feet to the camp where we arrived soaked to the skin. The porters, with their loads, had made it before us; the tents were up and a brew was on!

I dived in with Joy for a while, thankful for the warmth of her one dry pile jacket, grabbed out of her kitbag, and waited anxiously for Susie, John and Helen to get in. Somewhere along the line in our misery we'd been separated, and I was relieved to see them file in, weak, cold, sullen – but surviving.

John proceeded, as usual, to get us all into our sleeping bags and rushed about in the pouring rain, filling hot-water bottles and arranging for food to be brought to our tents. I dreaded having to go outside again, but the disquieting headaches were niggling away all the time, so I had to keep drinking. Happily, we had discovered that the collapsible washing bowls we brought with us this time made perfect peepots and I decided that John would just have to turn the other way and turn up the Walkman: no time for the niceties of life now. I stuffed wet clothes down my sleeping bag beside my body in an effort to dry them – just the smaller things like inner socks, knickers and balaclava. The bigger things, like trousers, jackets and expedition rain gear, hung from the tent poles on makeshift hooks or lay over our mud-caked bags, which were hard up to the sleeping bags. Helen and Susie's tent was door to door with ours again, so that we could call out to each other. Susie's knee was quite swollen and painful. It was a worrying injury to have, with days of strenuous walking ahead.

At six in the evening and after sixty-eight hours of monsoon madness, the porters, as ever, were heroic, bringing round soup, curried potatoes, pumpkin, rice and pudding. Some of the group stayed down by the porters' fire under the tarpaulin, talking and laughing – but we four tried to make our little nests comfortable and snuggled into our bags for warmth, having run out of energy.

John and I settled ourselves down nicely, and started to feel some of Doug's life forces flowing back into our bodies. Nicely, that is, apart from the fact that I was nervous about where the tent was pitched. It was on the edge of a steep drop and, in all this rain, I imagined slices of land sliding down the cliff quietly in the night – taking our tent with them. That was another irony of the mountains: in all those miles of open space there were only a few suitable places to make camp, where there was good water.

John discovered that his down sleeping bag was wet inside – and we both cringed as he climbed into it. His face was distorted with discomfort and I fully expected him to make some remark about 'getting out of this stupid business and going back' any minute. But he didn't and, instead, fished out his chocolate box and we shared a Mars bar between us. Even half a Mars bar took on a new dimension of delight up in the mountains, and we relished every mouthful. We decided to take our sleeping tablets straight away – to settle down and end this awful day as soon as possible. It wasn't easy to sleep well at altitude, because of the rarefied atmosphere, and it was not uncommon, among trekkers, to take sleeping tablets. So I took one, and John took three.

We were just nodding off when Andy arrived at the tent. He had a message from the gang by the fire for John. They wanted him to go down and join them, to sample the Mumbu rum. John explicitly told him to 'Foxtrot Oscar,' saying, 'Thanks but no thanks.' He settled back into his wet bag, pulling it up over his face. Ten minutes later, Doug appeared at the tent, unzipped it, grabbed John's boots from outside, threw them in and said, jovially, that they wouldn't take 'no' for an answer and that they'd all come and get him out if he didn't get a move on. John's loquacious answer, highlighted by a few 'bugger off Scott's' and more 'Foxtrot Oscar's,' didn't deter Doug at all. He was determined! Importunity was a characteristic of top-class climbers I suspected, and he wasn't listening to any of John's protestations as he tossed his coat at him. There seemed to be nothing for it but to go, and Doug backed out of the tent on all fours threatening to return with reinforcements if John didn't go down soon. Eventually, John grudgingly decided that he'd have to go and, still muttering about 'stupid buggers', told Doug, whose head was stuck through the door, that he'd 'come in a minute'. I was rapidly burying myself deeper and deeper in my bag, just in case anybody got any ideas about others coming. 'Give you five minutes then, youth.' That was the final statement from Doug before he stomped off into the darkness and slashing rain.

I peeked up over my sleeping bag, when I thought it was safe, and looked in astonishment at John sitting straight up. I told him I thought he should go, three sleeping tablets or not, as the mere thought of Doug, *et al*, charging up and flaying about in the tent, covered in mud and rain and leeches, and bodily dragging John out, filled me with horror. I was relieved to hear him say that he 's'posed' he'd have to go. 'Poor John,' I thought (now that he said he was going), as I watched him drag on his wringing-wet, cold trousers, his boots and soggy jacket, because they were all so unpleasant. 'He'll be lucky if he doesn't get pneumonia,' I thought, as he crawled out of the tent, but then, when he'd gone, I shrugged my shoulders, snuggled back into my warm bag and smiled, thinking that boys would be boys. An hour or so later, he was back. 'Oh,' I said, pleased, 'that's good, you'll be glad to get back into bed, won't you? You'll soon be warm.'

'Not bloody likely,' he said, and started rummaging about in his rucksack for something. 'It's bloody magic down there,' he beamed. 'We're having a great time, singing, and dancing and drinking.'

'Dancing?'

'Well, you know what I mean, jigging about.'

'What are you drinking, then?'

'Oh, I don't know: *rakshi* or rum or anything that's going round. I think they're trying to get me pissed.' He continued to heave things out of the sack. And while I was saying that I thought they were doing a good job, especially as John hardly drinks, he called out excitedly, 'Ah, here it is! I didn't think I'd be able to find it.'

'What?'

'My song book!'

'Oh no, not all those rugger songs and stuff.'

'Yaah – great,' he said punching the air. 'Bloody magic.'

I couldn't help smiling and tutting. He really was a boy scout at heart, John – and he always had the right thing for the right job for the right occasion in his rucksack. It was like the Mary Poppins carpet bag, out of which he seemed to be able to produce almost anything, other than a rabbit, at any time.

Hours and hours later, he staggered back up the slope to our tent, with the help of Simon, who told me in the morning that he'd turfed him out of their tent when he came crawling in calling them 'Mags.' He was very jolly, and talked non-stop, and repeatedly, about it being 'bloody magic' and how he 'wouldn't have missed it for the world.'

He busied around the tent looking for the peepot, it being still pouring with rain, and then burrowed, carelessly, down into his damp bag. I thought how he'd probably just taken the best tranquil-lizer imaginable – fun – and anaesthetized his fatigue and recharged his batteries rather well.

In the morning he felt fine. Best night's sleep he'd had since he set out, he said. We began to wonder if there was the faintest glow of sunshine coming through the tent. I went to the door to see, and listened with delight to a bird singing high up in the pine trees, feeling a sense of recovery creep into my being, amazed at how the world looked better on a sunny morning. Perhaps it was a pretty campsite after all. I called out, 'How're you doing, girls?'

'Not good,' Susie replied glumly, and put her head out of the tent. 'Helen's having trouble breathing; she couldn't get her breath all night. We've been awake for hours.'

We had come up quickly to 13,000 feet over the Shipton La, and although we had slept at 12,500 feet, maybe it had been just too quick a transition for Helen, or for us for that matter. Susie also said her knee was still giving her a lot of pain.

We got into our wet clothes and staggered out, blinking in the unaccustomed sunlight; we found that most of the party-goers were up and in fine form, although Terry admitted to feeling a little bit delicate. Joan, however, was really down. She refused to go on, Joy said, and she couldn't get her out of bed; nor was she sure what the problem was, other than her seeming low. Typically, Susie, knee immediately forgotten, was off to Joan's tent, and with her own brand of revitalizing people's spirits, had her up and rallied in no time. We helped her pack her things, and she set cheerfully off up the hill.

This twelfth day was marginally kinder, being rain-free for the first two hours. The walking was almost pleasant. We made a steep drop down to the Barun river, and moved along all together over the rock fall which edged it. It was slippery and dangerous, and extremely unstable. Huge masses of earth continually broke away from the top edge, and rolled trees and boulders of every size down the slope to the river. It was hard, this boulder-walking, and easy to fall; it was also hard on Susie's knee. But she stood up to it well, and we hurried along as quickly as possible. It was still an hour and a half before we left the river bank.

Dorjee, Umtu and Bhom were kind and helpful, and during this strenuous part they took our backpacks. Later, however, after we'd reached the lovely, grassy, stable banks and begun the steady climb up, they hurried on, taking our packs and lunch with them. This was bad luck for Bryan, as he usually ate my cold chips, because he was always hungry, and I didn't like them because they were always stuck to the tissue paper they were wrapped in.

We did see a little of the flora and fauna on this day – and a couple of rock rats, but we also had some pretty frightening, hurtling waterfalls to get through. But Dorjee, Bhom and Umtu helped us through all of these, and held the brollies, because of course the rain had returned. Several times along the way we stopped in caves to shelter and discovered that Dr Brian had been asked by one of the porters to visit his brother, who lived in a cave and wasn't well. When they got there they found him dead, poor soul, all alone and so far from anyone.

It was either waterfalls or downpours all day, both very wetting, and so we trudged along, seeing only the flooded ground, because every footstep had to be watched. It was painful and exhausting. We had just clawed our way up a steep waterfall, surrounded by huge rhododendron trees, with the water flowing all around us, when I turned back and saw Helen following, clearly on autopilot. She was covered from head to toe in her blue waterproofs. Her lank backpack, running with water, slipped at an angle on her back and her soaked hair was stuck to her cold, pinched face as her body heaved in gasps of breath. Seeing I'd stopped, she automatically did the same and leaned on her stick.

I said, through laboured breathing, 'You look awful, Helen,' – and when she'd summoned up enough strength to look at me and speak, she said with a weary feebleness, 'You don't look great yourself,' and we started to laugh – at the inexplicable idiocy of the whole thing. And we laughed and we laughed and we laughed –

and we cried – and laughed – and cried and cried and laughed and could not control either, till we grew weak with hysteria. Tears of bitter humour merged with tears of continual strain and streamed down our faces. Water flowed everywhere, and we laughed at the tears, and cried at the black humour. Susie tried to stop us, we tried to stop ourselves – and John just moseyed on – confused by women. Reverse hysteria, I believe it's called, and we went through those paroxysms until we were completely spent.

Greg, Mark and Simon came by – and we all sat down in the mud and ate sweets and they smoked wet cigarettes and nobody cared about sitting in freezing mud on a mountainside, in the rain. 'Don't worry about it,' they said. They said they knew just how we felt. They'd cried lots of times on a mountain – sometimes it was the only thing to do, when things were bad, and they agreed that this weather was bad, the worst any of them had ever seen here. It made us feel better, being told that, being told that even tough climbers cried in severe conditions, and these were severe conditions. And so our bizarre, clarty little *tête-à-tête* in the cold rain proved to be extremely beneficial. But after seven hours of the hardest graft, we arrived at the camp like half-dead, drowned rats.

However, Nehe Kharka was the nicest spot we'd stayed in so far, with hundred-foot-high cliffs behind us and a racing river in front. The grassland was flat and felt safe, without the sense of danger one gets on the cliffy bits, and Joan made it, albeit very slowly, and seemed better.

We decided to stay in our tent for supper that night, not being able to face the continual regarbing in wet clothes, and though we'd started the day in a slightly better frame of mind, with the brief gleam of sunshine, the afternoon rain had ultimately washed away our bit of cheer. Now we just wanted to be warm and in bed.

While we were wondering how we'd managed to pick one of the worst monsoons ever, John replaced the batteries in his radio, hoping to get World Service. He always tried to get the English broadcast, but as he was not often successful, we weren't holding out much hope. So when, suddenly, Brian Johnston's mellifluous voice, commentating on the cricket from Lord's, pierced the air, it brought the brightest beam of nostalgia imaginable into our tired hearts, and gave us the biggest fillip possible. It filled the tent with home and John and I heaved huge, soppy sighs of longing. If ever we'd had a greater need for something homely, then I couldn't think what it could be; or of anything more evocatively English than cricket. I would never have believed that one day I'd find the unemotional cricket commentary so overwhelmingly emotional – or that it would make my heart soar. But it did and we hung on to every word as Henry Blofeld, presumably wearing his bow tie, told us that the skies were a beautiful blue, that they were sitting in their shirtsleeves in warm sunshine, and that England was batting in reply to Sri Lanka's 194. When he said that Warwickshire (our home team) was playing Worcestershire, it brought such a lump to our throats that we could barely listen to any more and we just looked at each other, filled with emotion. 'Oh, Mags,' John said and could say no more. He didn't need to – I felt the same.

Was it really a lovely, hazy English summer day at home, with bumblebees buzzing, and people in flannels and straw hats clapping politely from their deck chairs and snoozing between the 'ow zats' – and will there be honey still for tea?

It was cricket that rocked the cradle that night in the high Himal – hard to imagine, but true.

6

The Reaper Harvests

Brian, the doctor, rushed around the tents at 5.30 on the eleventh morning, calling to us to look out of our tents. There, against a clear blue sky, snow-capped and magnificent, was Makalu.

We were amazed, not realizing that we were in sight of it, and delighted that our endurance of the last eleven days of monsoon conditions, leeches and earthquakes had paid off. And here was our reward: Makalu, towering theatrically against the sky in the distance, inspiring us to go on. All around us were juniper thickets, glossy green rhododendrons, soaring pines and sparkling streams, a sylvan scene – with no rain!

We threw the tent open, and the rotting socks out, relieved at last to get rid of some of the smell and perhaps, some of the wet. For almost the first time since Tumlingtar, we sat outside to eat breakfast. What a joy to hear the birds singing and to see the mountains, to breathe in the brisk, clean air and to set off in warm filtered sunshine! A joy to walk through fern-filled rocky outcrops seeing, at last, yellow and pink cotoneaster, blue, white and purple sweet peas and miniature delphiniums. And it was Andy Watts's birthday.

Even up at 14,000 feet there are pastures, and though the growth is considerably stunted by the cold it seemed to sustain a few goats and yaks. These are not pure yaks (mountain ox) but *az's*, or *adz's* according to the dialect, and come somewhere between the eight stages of a cow and a yak. Many of the original yaks were driven out of the border lands of Nepal and Tibet by the Chinese. These small herds were shepherded by cave dwellers. We caught sight of the occasional coil of smoke drifting up from caves in the cliffs, and of the wild dogs which prowled around the entrances. We'd been thinking what an incredibly lonely life it must be when, right up at 15,000 feet, we came upon a proper stone house with a reed roof and a walled vegetable garden, full of vegetables, especially spinach. A tribe of children tumbled out of the smoke-filled home on hearing us. We sampled some of the family's goat yoghurt, which was cool and a bit sharp. The father greeted Doug warmly, remembering him from previous years on his way up to Makalu, and Doug stayed with them while we pressed on.

We were never sure how much farther our goal was, but we idled along because one had to go slowly at this altitude – and because it wasn't raining. There was a considerable degree of sickness throughout the group: Nigel was particularly sick with some sort of fever, and Joan struggled, plagued by the altitude, but she took Diamox daily which, though it makes your fingers tingle, seemed to help her. Her greatest uplift, however, was nineteen-year-old Bhom. They had found an empathy, and struck up a very jolly friendship. Bhom would teach her Nepalese words, and she would teach him English 'ditties', translated by Dorjee. '*Pearre*', Bhom told her, is Nepalese for 'darling', which was one of Joan's favourite terms of endearment, and one could often hear her laughing out loud when she walked with Bhom.

We stopped to eat our apple, egg and cold chips; Andy Parkin even settled down to make some drawings, so improved was the weather. We talked about Andy's birthday, about how we should do something at dinner that night perhaps, something to make it special.

Some evenings, after dinner, John took it upon himself to read poetry to us. He was the vicar, dispensing spiritual uplift and replenishing moral fibre, but we weren't a very receptive throng. We had been so tired, fed up and lethargic up to then that we'd never been able to summon up enough energy to dissuade him – so mostly we just sat there, checking leeches, dripping and just, well, half listening – humouring him really. But in a roundabout sort of way I liked it, because he read Pam Ayres and her poetry reminded me of my two sons, Greg and Guy. My eldest son, Greg, can recite Pam Ayers verbatim and even ad nauseam, and I would sit there listening to John reciting those familiar words, and drift off hearing Greg tossing her lines into all sorts of everyday situations, with Guy doing the ad libs – 'like you would'. Perhaps it was therapeutic, after all. It made me think of how they would tease me about 'my love, peace and vegetable rights', as they called it, and I imagined what fuel this would give to their humour if they could see me now: a ragged vegetarian, member of a bunch of transient friends stuck up a mountain in a monsoon – dogged with a litany of rain, pain and sickness. At times like that, I thought, a dose of their joshing would have done me a power of good since one can never quite outrun the shadow of home. We decided to make Andy a card and to give him a present: a big present, like a whole sweetie or two – or something really generous, like one of our matchbox-sized boxes of Smarties.

Susie volunteered to make the card as long as someone else wrote the verse. They scanned around and lighted on me. I puffed, 'Don't look at me; I can't write verse.'

'Yah – you can – you do it, Mags,' they said, neatly tossing the ball in my court and extricating themselves.

'Well I think we should all think about it on the trail,' I said. 'After all, we've got plenty of time' – it was another seven-hour day – 'What about Steve? He's the one with a first in maths at Oxford – or Simon, with an hons, or something; he ought to be able to write verse.'

But Steve, who was always charmingly reticent about his prowess, said with a modest shrug that he was 'just good at sums, that's all!' A remark that we thought should go in the annals as one of the great understatements of the trek – next to John's, of course, saying that it might be *a bit wet!* Helen, head down, lips pursed, remained blithely untroubled by such things as verse writing.

But fortunately it just came into my head. We'd always had a lot of jokes from day one with Welsh Andy and Simon, and a few about the great size of Simon (Andy called him Bear) or a subject dear to most men's hearts: the relative size of hands and feet to the dangly bits. Life gets very basic in the mountains. And though Andy insisted that Simon's six-foot-three, sixteen-stone body might indicate something about Simon, Andy's own size didn't accurately indicate anything about him, and he often joked about taking only a size seven shoe, which obviously wasn't true. So I knew there had to be something there to write about.

Bhom came to call us for dinner, and Susie, who'd been energetically around the tents in the pouring rain (it had started again) to collect all the trekkers' signatures for the card made out of the soggy back of an exercise book, was trying to finish it. Helen took an interest in the proceedings from her bed, interjecting with the odd blinding insight, but that seemed to tire her somewhat so there weren't many. She said it had been a hard day. It had, especially the last two or three hours. Coming to this camp called Mera, alongside the ever cracking Barun glacier, was quite a marathon.

All of us were in one mess tent for Andy's party dinner. Thirty-seven, I counted, which made it extremely crushed, but jolly. The porters brought in a wonderful cake, iced with the words 'Happy Birthday Andy', which was no doubt Sharu's work, and really quite remarkable under the circumstances. The presentation began. The poem, courtesy of many a similar rhythm, went like this.

Dear Andy – on this special day
We think that we can truthfully say
We've climbed up some mountains, though not many we've seen
And braved all the leeches, and forded some streams
We've crossed over bridges, that give you the jitters
And drunk too much *rakshi*, which gives you the squitters
We've not had a day, when we've been really dry
Thanks to a monsoon that would make a man cry
And we've taken the tablets – enough to fell an ox
Just to bring you – this box – of chocs (hand over box)
But most of all – we survived the earthquake
This birthday card for you to make.
And so we leave you with love and affection
And hope that you get a size seven . . . birthday cake!

Andy enjoyed his party.

As we walked back by torchlight to our tent across the rocky edge of the glacier I looked for my Great Bear, my little constellation and reference point. I began to get quite dejected about not ever seeing it on this trip, knowing that, if I did, just once in clear, starry skies, that would perhaps mean a change in the weather and banish the eternal rain. But no luck. 'Bear be there,' I whispered, 'we need you.'

Another sleepless night followed, with raging headaches and a bleeding nose, and I woke feeling wretched. I couldn't wait to get to base camp that day, then possibly ABC? – then to go down out of the rain.

But base camp was not to be, since on this twelfth morning Helen was sick, really sick, with a pounding head, from debilitating diarrhoea and the altitude. She was too sick to go on.

Susie and I had one of our strategic meetings, by the loo tent, and since we had learnt by now not to press on regardless, and that with a porter and cook-boy we could stay put, we decided we should do just that. But as we watched all the others pack up to go, we mulled over the coincidence of each one of us reining back on the day of base camp. At Everest it had been me; K2 Susie; and now it was Helen at Makalu. But there was nothing for it, and once we'd relieved Helen of the fear of having to go on, and Dr Brian had prescribed rest, she settled down deep into her sleeping bag, with a hot-water bottle, pursed lips, and slept. Now would we get to BC? And what about ABC? The ambition of the 21,000-foot crampon climb now looked disappointingly doubtful.

Susie and I were pleased when Andy (Norris) told us that Rick and Alison Allen were staying down as well since they both had extremely bad colds.

It was a cold, miserable, monochrome day with the dreary, black loo-tent door flapping, its toilet paper lying soaked in the mud; and the barren glacier behind, grey and ominous, exploded frighteningly all the time with avalanches. First it cracked like lightning, and then rumbled like thunder as the snow fell down its steep edge – a constant reminder of the power of the elements.

In the late afternoon I took a stroll out of the camp, and surveyed the scene in disbelief. Could it be that forsaken, friendless little tent set in such wet, rocky isolation, was our only refuge? We'd come a long way from our kitchen sinks now, and just about as far from the hermetically sealed holidays and the comfortable lives we knew as it was possible to be – and though we weren't quite alone, it looked, and felt, as if we were. I understood now what courage it had taken for someone like Alexandra David-Neel, and the other women travellers, to explore these mountains alone in the early part of this century.

And were we really happy? All the questions about climbers could be asked about ourselves. If it was adventuring we wanted, we certainly had that. Here we were, a few kilometres from the Tibetan border, 16,500 feet up, our only protection a tent, one of us not well, twelve days' hard walk up from Tumlingtar and alone – apart from two other sick people and a cook-boy who didn't speak English. We didn't like what we saw in the mirror, our eyes were swollen, our lips cracked and broken, and our skin like leather. We were suffering from head colds and heart-stopping sneezes. Our noses bled, our hair was unwashed (other than by rain), and our bowels were in turmoil. The food we ate, though excellent was . . . *different*. Even the men, I'd thought this morning for the first time, looked drawn, tired and unkempt. The only good thing was the obvious, and dramatic, weight loss, but having your teeth wired together might be easier, and a lot less painful. And had we learnt anything? Yes, we'd learnt endurance and how to wrestle with one's willpower to keep on enduring, and persevering, in order to achieve and survive. And were we happy? Yes, I think we were happy within ourselves. So far we'd proved to be pretty tough and very able up to this point, I thought. I only had to look at Helen and Susie to see that; and one couldn't help but be enormously stimulated by the experiences and by the friends we had made. For sure, the kitchen sink would never look the same again and I only wished I'd done it earlier.

We took our opium of trekking in a huge dollop that night, by hanging a torch on the tent pole, snuggling down like peas in a pod, and talking and talking and talking. We swore we'd never, ever, come again – during the monsoon. A pale moon shone through the clouds, a wild dog howled in the darkness, and I prayed: 'Bear, please, be there and bring us a little bit of sunshine tomorrow.'

My prayer was answered, eventually, and we got there, on the thirteenth day, to base camp. Tough old Hen pulled round, and we waited for the porters to come down from base camp for us. We were pleased with the thought that we could set our own pace that day, as there was unquestionably an unspoken challenge about pace, albeit unintentional, with a group of macho men, and at last we experienced the first lovely day's walking and saw the grandeur of the scenery. The sun shone, the birds sang and we smelled the flowers. We looked at the butterflies and talked and laughed, in sign and pidgin, with our porters. They'd often called us three women *brias*. As they came to the tent, particularly in the mornings with the tea, they would say, 'Good morning, *Bria*, tea ready' and finally I asked Prem, who spoke English, 'What is *bria*?'

I wished I hadn't asked him, as we learnt to our chagrin that it meant old lady – really old lady, crippled-with-a-stick old lady, if their unnecessarily, overly explicit actions were anything to go by and the way they fell about laughing. We feigned a bit of annoyance at this, and they loved it, as we loved them for their kindness and support. We loved both the fresh lemon juice they made for us, which was quite *meta* (delicious) and their *chiyaa* (tea). They pointed out Makalu, telling us that the word meant mother.

When we watched a rock rat eating with its paws, unperturbed by our presence, and pulled on our scarves, Arab-style, to shade the sun, I thought about how understandable it was that the sun was worshipped as a god in some parts of the world; it has such an uplifting effect. It dispelled our worst fears and changed our whole perspective on things, and things didn't look as bad that day. I even started to believe we'd finished battling with the elements and looked forward just to being able to enjoy a satisfying level of exercise during the day's walk, without detrimental exhaustion. Was the penance done? I began to wonder – but I should have known better than that.

We took the last thousand feet easy and, as we rounded a bluff, suddenly, a long way in the distance, across the Barun river far below, was the base camp. It was set in a green pasture next to the river and, as we walked down towards the river, they spotted us, waved shirts, banged things and called out. We danced about with joy. Makalu base camp!

But always the caveat. John came out to fetch us. He must have walked a mile, bringing little chocolate bars, a bear hug and news. Unfortunately, it made me suspicious; I feared an ulterior motive.

'The bridge – it's not great,' he said. 'But we'll get you over.'

'Is it really bad, then?' I asked nervously.

'Well, like I say, it's not good.' he winced. 'Bhom fell off it yesterday.'

'What?' we shrieked.

'It's OK, it's OK. He's all right. They had a rope slung across the river to hold on to – and he hung on to it, thank goodness. The river is pretty fast and it washed him downstream – but Andy ran down the bank and somehow they hauled him in. Pretty nasty with a pack on your back!'

'Poor Bhom,' Susie said, with deep concern, speaking for us all.

'Yes, 'fraid so – it scared him, he's very shaken.'

As we approached the bridge – well, a log, really, looking round, wet and slippery to me – you could see how it had happened. This, we assumed, was the bridge that the Frenchman had told us was down. However, it did have a rail fixed on to one side and it wasn't high off the water, four or five feet that's all. Andy waited downstream. Greg and Alan Hinckes stood over the far side, with cameras, and over we all went. Helen never had any problems with bridges, and Susie was only marginally perturbed.

As soon as we got into camp, delighted to be reunited with our buddies, Susie was off to see Bhom. He'd taken a load up to ABC that morning and now he was tucked up in a tent, not looking good. But Brian was there looking after him, and his uncle, one of the porters, was burning some incense outside his tent on a stone. Nigel was also in bed; he appeared to be much worse. He hadn't eaten for days now and was in a deep fever, possibly flu. Everyone else seemed to be in tolerably good health and although the severe diarrhoea was very dehydrating, I was pleased to see that young Bryan, who had suffered this the most, was in good form.

There was a general buzz of excitement through the camp, over-looked by Makalu and Tutsi, because they hoped to go to the great goal in the sky tomorrow: ABC. We decided not to go. We weren't acclimatized well enough to go up to twenty-odd thousand feet – it just wouldn't have been sensible and, anyway, we were tired. There was plenty of attraction in resting at BC for us, and lots of enjoyment in their excitement.

It was a delightful morning, the fourteenth, and we flitted about the group watching as they packed up their backpacks, ice axes and crampons and prepared to get off. It was particularly good to see John off on this last great adventure – he'd been thinking about it for so long. Only a handful stayed behind: Terry ('I think I'll go to my chambers and read some papers!'), Rick, Alison and Kirsten. Mark, Simon and Greg left casually about midday. But all the trekkers, except Nigel, got away with Doug and the other climbers, early. Joan, who had been suffering for days now, found renewed energies; and Reg, who had told us about having some sort of shaking fit or spasm for five minutes in the night, and was extremely quiet and anxious at breakfast, was equally determined to go up.

It was an excited departure, with hugs and kisses and lingering waves till they had finally disappeared. They walked out along the river bed and up towards Makalu; to who knew what, we pondered, as we sat in an almost pastoral scene with no snow, or rain, or leeches, and excitedly speculated about their next two or three days. We would never have been able to foresee ours.

The skeleton group left behind were all busy doing domestics. We girls, crazed with excitement, washed and sun-dried our clothes and hair, and took siestas, knowing it had been decided to go down to Tumlingstar in only eight days, which was bound to be a hard journey. Then Reg staggered back into the camp – utterly exhausted. He told us how the first part had been very tough indeed. Not only had it been hard going, over extremely rocky terrain, but they'd come to a 600-foot wall – and though Reg had known that the climbing would have to be steep to go up 3,000 feet, when it came to the wall he just didn't have the strength to go any further. A porter had brought him back. Andy and Joy were going really well, he said, and the others slowly, but OK. I worried about them sleeping high that night – and about how they would be the next day. We hoped to take a little walk ourselves to have a look at Everest and

Lhotse, if it was clear. Bhom wasn't much better. Maybe it was flu. Nigel thought he had flu. Susie took drinks in to them both regularly and Dr Brian was still there, at BC, watching over them.

During the night I awoke, shocked and frightened by a bad dream. I dreamt that I saw our friends clustered around something, obviously concerned. I walked over to see what it was they were looking at and as I came near they parted and I saw someone lying on the ground, someone very ill, or dead, I wasn't sure, but then I saw that it was Bryan, young Bryan, my walking mate Bryan, and I worried.

I hated this business of sleeping on my own, because I dreamt too much, but then I remembered that it was a fact that the age group most vulnerable to altitude sickness was nineteen to twenty-five. This seems rather peculiar, but it's probably because they are apt to travel quickly, being fitter. I told myself to stop worrying. It was only a dream. But still I would be very glad to see them all safely back.

I was also glad when I heard Umtu at 4.30, coming to the tent with the tea and breaking my train of thought – until I saw that he was in an agitated state. He explained hurriedly that they had to take Bhom down the mountain quickly, straight away as he was very sick. 'Wo go now,' he said – and Susie, hearing this from her tent, was out like a shot to Bhom.

Brian was with him. Nigel, having heard Bhom's uncle calling his nephew's name between 3.30 and 4.00, had dragged himself out of his tent and found Bhom's uncle holding his hand and urgently intoning prayers, while Bhom struggled to breathe. He called Brian. Immediately, Brian gave him a diuretic injection, and mouth-to-mouth resuscitation. But tragically, at 5.50, Bhom died, of pulmonary oedema.

'Bhom dead,' we cried, dumbfounded. 'Bhom?'

Susie nodded in confirmation. That bright, laughing, kind, caring nineteen-year-old boy – dead.

'How? How could it be?'

'Altitude sickness – pulmonary oedema,' Susie said. We slumped back in silence.

We sat in the mess tent with Bryan, Terry and Nigel, all of us in a state of shock, trying to comprehend what had happened, deciding what to do. I couldn't help but reflect soberly on my dream. Was it Bhom I saw then? And by what slender thread had I held on at Everest? Again I thought that, but for Pemba, I wouldn't have been here to mourn for Bhom.

We'd cried a lot over the three trips, but, peculiarly now we were too stunned, too bewildered, too remorseful to cry. If anything, we marvelled at the porters and cook-boys and their philosophical approach to Bhom's death. They had their Buddhism now to help them – their belief in reincarnation, their commitment to not killing any living creature, as it was someone reincarnated; and their peace now lay in knowing that Bhom would be reincarnated. They believed that Bhom's spirit would return as a bird or an animal or some finer form, maybe even attain the perfect state – Nirvana – and this gave them strength. But what had we? Nothing much more than non-spiritual thoughts and materialism, all of which seemed rather inadequate.

A liaison officer came during the day from the nearby Spanish expedition, and he and Terry legally recorded the death. A detailed report (written with pages out of my diary) had to go back to a government office, as an expedition is responsible for all of its members, including the porters. A runner was sent up to ABC with the news for Doug, and as we sat in our tent, waiting for this to be done, we talked about Joan, knowing she would be devastated.

About 2.30, it started to rain and Dorjee came to the tent to borrow the rain gear. They were digging the grave. It overlooked the river. Late in the greyest of afternoons, the porters carried Bhom's body, wrapped in a blanket, slowly through the swirling mist and rain to the grave. They buried him there, in what seemed to us the saddest, loneliest, most windblown and rain-spattered bed. It was a heart-breaking sight – but he had with him his stick and his bundle of possessions for the long journey, and his uncle and friends knew he was going to a better world.

7

Nothing like a Dame

OUR climbers filtered back into the camp two and three at a
time, eyes sad with the news, bodies roughened and jaded by
their exertions. Joan, terribly upset, smiled weakly and asked
bemused questions. Then she went on to tell us how she'd had a
strange experience herself. Apparently, up on the mountain, she'd
thought she'd seen Bhom coming towards her, and had actually
called out to the others, 'Hey up, here's my little Bhom' – and then
he wasn't there. They'd thought it funny at the time, and she'd
dismissed it herself quickly, feeling strangely chilled – but she was
cconvinced she'd seen him.

Call it telepathy, empathy, intuition – what you will – but there
did appear to be a magnification of the senses up in the mountains.
We seemed to be more emotional, and were sensitive to the slightest
nuance in ourselves and others. We'd shed our worldly possessions,
and I wondered if, in this unconscious stripping of ourselves to the
bone, people for people's sake so to speak, we didn't touch on the
more spiritual quality of our lives. And maybe some were more
receptive than others. Even Buddhist monks vary, some being more
transcendental and attuned to the inner self than others. But it did
seem undeniable that there was a heightened awareness about others,
and for some of us these incidents weren't just imagination – they
were genuine insight. I'm sure Joan saw Bhom. I saw Bhom – or
was it Bryan?

Joan went to see Bhom's grave, to say goodbye to her friend. His
coat and brolly, just below the stones, brought him flooding back
to her and intensified the pathos. Her little Bhom dying of altitude
sickness! How could this happen to a man of the mountains? It is
a fact that these mountain people also have to acclimatize, expecially
if they come from the lower villages – and Bhom of course came in
that vulnerable age bracket. In his eagerness to work well, he probably sped on too quickly.

However, it is a little soothing to think that by next spring that simple grave will bloom with wild flowers and the scrub grass – manifesting Bhom's spirit, which, like the flowers, will be part of the great mountains forever.

The gang's stories of being on Makalu were endless. The 600-foot wall had daunted them all. And then I learnt that the steepness of the climb on up to ABC had taken its toll with Bryan, that the altitude had affected him badly and kept him at ABC while the others pressed on – extrasensory perception?

The rest pushed on and got to 20,500 feet on a small peak. In their excitement, they gave it their own name – Trekksi. It obviously took a great deal of determination, and they'd done battle royal with fatigue – but the climbers were superb, they said. Guiding and encouraging all the way, they'd almost literally dragged the trekkers up the last thousand feet. Roped together one to one, they had continually checked the trekkers' crampons and shown them how to heave themselves up with the ice axes. They'd even cut ice steps for them, which is an extremely strenuous task, at twenty thousand feet, and having finally reached their peak, a great camaraderie had grown between them – everyone sharing the success. John, like the others, was deliriously happy about the climb, not least of all because he had been higher than Mount McKinley – which was his next goal. He couldn't find the words to describe the sensation and satisfaction he was feeling – or the words to describe the way it felt to stand close to the top of this mighty crown of mountains: to look across and see Mount Everest (ten miles away), Llosthe and Makalu – the world – but it showed in his eyes and was etched deep into his heart.

In the evening we gathered together for what would have been the last night's *soirée* but of course now it was something of a wake. John spoke first, in his usual easy manner, and relived the awful walk-in, saying that 'it was bloody 'orrible and never again' – but at the end of the day, things had all come really good for them on the hill – and Doug had given him the finest hour of his life.

Then Doug spoke of Bhom, reminding us what an incredible impression this nineteen-year-old lad had made in just a few days and how he'd made our journey so much more pleasant with his winning ways – and that we would probably remember him long after we got back home. That in the face of his death our achievements seemed light, perhaps even pointless, and that while it was important for us to reach out and stretch ourselves to achieve our own personal best we must not do it with blinkers on, looking only forward. We must learn to watch out for those who played the supporting role and helped us to gain, and to care and to take them along with us. For gain at others' expense is no accolade to wear proudly and unless we'd earned our achievements honourably and fairly then they could not be admired.

It was 11.30 when we went to bed, the latest so far, and as the joky callings across the dark camp, of 'night, John boy,' 'night, Peter' etc rang out from the torchlit tents Big Ben's chimes also rang out from John's radio. It brought to mind John Donne's pertinent verse – any man's death diminishes me, and therefore never send to know for whom the bell tolls, it tolls for thee! It was strange how fate had made this day their zenith and our nadir.

In the morning we heard one of the porters call out to Joan as she crossed the camp, 'Good morning DARLING!' It was a bitter-sweet reminder – but it felt right and proper.

This was the leaving day – and ironically I woke feeling really well and strong, and although the heart-stopping sneezes and the constant nose bleed hadn't gone, I thought I'd finally acclimatized and could have gone on up today. Sod's law I suppose – because it was down we had to go. I always seemed to be a day late and a dollar short, with this trekking, but at least I knew now that I could go farther than I would ever have believed. However, we were not all going down unreadily, though, as Nigel and Reg especially were not well and we had a long hike ahead of us.

Cameras clicked with dozens of team photos and we parted warmly with the climbers, knowing that they had all, along with the porters, done their utmost to help us realize our goals. They'd made us persevere when we'd stumbled, made us stretch out, strive for more, and pushed us on to achieve our ambitions and done everything in their power to help us enjoy the trip – and we all appreciated that. But, most of all, we realized how much we admired them. They'd opened our eyes to mountaineering, and we saw the kind of courage it takes to climb big mountains – and we saw that the courage required is so far beyond most people's conception of courage that we'd never be able fully to appreciate it.

We left them to their colossal undertaking. It would be a couple of months before we heard how they'd fared in the awesome arms of Mount Makalu, and we'd be anxiously waiting to hear that they were all safely off the hill.

The morning was lovely. We girls were refreshed by the rest, the others were stimulated by their climb, and we felt that there was nothing we couldn't handle today as we hiked off into the sunshine. We had lunch at the yak herder's hut and lay in the meadow while Dorjee bought spinach and potatoes from the shepherd. All was going well till it started again – the rain, torrential rain – and eight hours later, soaked to the skin, cold, miserable, anaesthetized with disbelief that it wasn't over – we staggered into Nehe Kharka.

Now Helen had a letter; she'd had it with her all the time. Her husband had written it to her and given it to her to open when she was at the top, or whenever she was at her lowest and needed a bit of bolstering. Many times Susie and I had tried to get her to open it, at bad times coming up, but she didn't think she could face it yet, suggesting that it might just about bring on the emotional overload – and that she couldn't take any more. But this night she couldn't have been lower, or nearer to tears, with the prospect of facing more endless days of rain – so a few more wouldn't make any difference. She opened it, read it, blubbed and passed it to us. He told her how proud he was of her. How his dearest wish was for her to do whatever would bring her the greatest sense of achievement and satisfaction, that he wanted her to do whatever it took for her to achieve it – and that he loved her. We gave it back to her and told her to put it away quickly – we couldn't cope with the emotion either.

Martha (Doug's daughter) came back with us. She had to be back at school by mid-September and when I nipped into her tent the following morning just before breakfast I found her troubled and distressed and was surprised to learn that she was terrified about her father climbing Makalu. She had convinced herself, the way one does in the dark hours of the night, that something was going to happen to him. Because he was slightly doubtful about getting to the summit (only because of the weather – as so much rain down here could mean avalanche conditions on the mountain), his negativeness, as she saw it, would be his undoing and put his life at risk. I talked to her – telling her that it wasn't true. Doug was infallible, he was not one of the mose experienced mountaineers in the business for nothing, and his own intuitive caution wouldn't allow him to do anything that would endanger his life. Hey – this is Doug Scott we're talking about, Mr Dependable, Mr Mountain Goat, who's clung to more mountainsides, for thirty years, than she could imagine, and that there was no way anything was going to happen to him. But Martha was only fifteen, and she had hated leaving him, and was tortured by her heightened emotions and sorely in need of his comfort. But she was nothing if not the daughter of Doug Scott, and though she sniffed quietly all the way through her porridge at breakfast, the reassurance made her feel better and she set off strong and cheery as usual, disappearing into the mist.

At lunch, in a cave out of the rain, Helen's morale revived fractionally when Simon spoon-fed her with the Sherpa stew, which was obviously deemed necessary by Andy (trek leader) to see us through another blockbuster of a day. Helen had stopped eating properly days previously. When it rains incessantly and you haven't got much meat on your bones, you get very cold, and your psyche plummets and you start to lose your fight.

Nigel battled on but looked terrible; he must have lost two stone. He said it was recurring malaria, but I thought it was all altitude-related myself. Joan was still taking Diamox. Susie's legs, knees and ankles all hurt – 'Otherwise I'm in great shape,' she said with crushing sarcasm. 'I've lost weight where I don't want to – her bust – I look about ninety, and have developed leg muscles like a porter. Get me to Kathmandu.'

Anyway, somehow we braved out the next day for nine hours. The cold rain stung our faces like sharp needles all day and I'll never know how we made it. We didn't stop for lunch or tea and briefly ate our cold chips and *purrie* (bread) sitting on a rock with the rain running down us like a drainpipe and flowing into the gushing stream. As if that weren't enough, the vine-strangled rhododendrons delivered fat blobs of water down our necks, and the rain plastered our trousers coldly to our legs. Even *I* ate the chips that day; Bryan, who usually ate mine, had long disappeared in the watery undergrowth. I tried not to dwell on the fact that we were heading back into leech country. When we'd set out we'd joked about 'letting the agony begin' and surely it did, step by cold, agonizing step. Up over the Shipton La and through the boggy edges of the lakes. Over misty expanses of rock, rock and rock, through boulder-strewn streams, through thick woods and sprawling roots, hoods up, heads down, eyes closed to anything but the muddy path and the clarty boots of the person in front. I wondered if the curtain of bone-chilling rain would ever open – and worried about Helen. Would she make it? She was snappish and irrational and looking a bit blue, and at one point told Andy, who always stayed with us, crossly that 'this was so incredibly hard that even her sons couldn't do it'. It was the only thing that made me smile all day, because as I followed her wet shape I thought of them – all three. Two who were in their twenties were six-foot-one rugger playing tornadoes, and the third, a rapidly sprouting fifteen-year-old, wasn't far behind! I knew I'd be able to remind her of this peevish comment some time in the future, and that she'd laugh about it then.

But, nevertheless, as we came into the eighth hour I was past caring myself and about finding words for it all. Maybe Helen was right. Her sons would have found it difficult, and if she got through it she'd be pretty damned good herself. We would all have done well.

The reception we gave to Dorjee and Umtu, coming up the mountainside with a kettle of hot tea and biscuits and telling us that the camp was only fifteen minutes away, must have made them feel positively saintly. And although it proved to be forty minutes, we barely noticed – as suddenly it was warmer. Wonderfully warmer. And by the time we got to Tashigoan we were steaming.

We took plenty of the *rakshi* with supper that night, and after resuming the dreaded 'leech deplete' slept in the schoolroom with our brollies over our sleeping bags. Dorjee told us that some of Doug's porters had been enticed away from our expedition by the Spanish, and he'd had to send more men up to Doug.

There is an axiom in weaving which says that 'a thread under tension is a thread under control' but now I know that a nerve under tension is a nerve out of control and that's how it was for the next two days. We'd met our Waterloo. We hated Kauma, hated Mumbuk, hated Seduwa – loved the villagers – loathed the leeches, didn't like the wet tents, hated the mountains and detested the monsoon with a passion. We really just couldn't quite believe it.

But we'd learned to bend a knee at the might of the mountains. To respect the indomitable power of the elements which had thrown everything at our little caravan of misery and driven us scuttling down through the folds of the mountains in search of safe haven day after day. We learnt some humility as our safety-net tent-talks seemed to lose some of their profundity – and all that psychologizing about learning something about ourselves seemed like no more than regurgitated pap now. And we saw how the hard days blinded us to the good ones, until we left Num on the twenty-first day, that was – when it didn't rain ALL DAY! Then, we were quite fickle and responsive to the charms of the sunshine, and the path we took through the mountains started to look, well, rather lovely, beautiful even.

At last, after nearly twenty-one days, it felt as if we were coming out of the darkness – into the light. Just strolling into the camp (not scrabbling around desperately to get into a tent), and chatting to the villagers, some of whom spoke a little English, was like coming into the light. Having drier clothes and leechless tents was coming into the light, and drinking beer and *chi* outside was coming into the light. John, having brought balloons for the children and making them squeal with pleasure, this was a delight; suddenly things were all right with our little world!

Finally we'd ridden the storm. From now on it would be a smooth and sunny passage. We were so glad, having got a bit tired by the troughs of despair and peaks of euphoria. The next three days down to Tumlingtar would be wonderful – and Bear would be there!

The children had John out of his tent at dawn, back in strength for the balloons, and they batted them around us as we ate fresh village eggs for breakfast under a blue sky. On the way down through the terraces we saw the whole ecological scene. Jack and the Beanstalk sized beans, wild tomatoes, vines, cucumbers, marrows, bananas, pears, water buffaloes, goats, kids, pigs and piglets. Rock rats and crickets, black butterflies and monkeys, paddy fields, soya beans, lentils, spinach and the staple crop: potatoes. There were terraces, as far as you could see, carved in long sweeping curves over the mountain slopes at harmony with the land. There was timber and water! Dung for fuel, rush for roofs, rush for mats – rush for plates and rush for hats – all bathed in sunlight.

We got down to the Arun river and then, dripping only in perspiration, huffed and puffed our way back up the other side for 2,500 feet to the village of Ahale. We washed our feet and socks under the village tap, and chatted to the schoolteacher. A lady asked us if we would sponsor her son, and put him through school, which we thought an interesting proposition, but didn't take it up. The leeches were noticeably fewer and we were really happy about that. It may be that, like the monsoon, their season was ending – we certainly hoped so.

Susie slept in with Joan, and we could hear them talking without drawing breath. We didn't need a degree in rocket science to guess that they were talking about leeches!

In the morning Joy was in high dudgeon because her boots had been stolen. At first she was convinced it was one of the fellas mucking about, but it really wasn't and we had to accept that they had been 'borrowed' but probably not by the locals. Luckily, she had another pair of boots to carry on with. Normally, at this stage trainers are all right as the paths are easier, as was the weather, which improved every few hundred feet we dropped. At one point, when we were resting at a tea house in the sun, two men came running down the path, carrying a body on a stretcher. An old man indicated that they were taking it to the river for burial. The Tibetans have another method: they cut the body open and leave it on the grass for the vultures to take away the spirit and aid reincarnation.

And we saw Helen's spirits lift like a metamorphosis in her. Whether it was Andy (Watts) flitting around the girls, giving us all a heady whiff of his fresh shaving lotion – or the opiate for her of shopping at Khandbari tomorrow, we couldn't be sure – but she went down that path with wings on her heels. Having dragged her up the hill, we now couldn't keep up with her, going down. She sped on, with what spur we knew not, unless it was a guardian shopper that had her by the hand – and we watched her change from a joyless blob to a sparkling bubble.

Susie never changed. Even when she was tired she was as cheerful as could be expected under the circumstances and, she never failed to be supportive to others. She pressed on also, wanting nothing more than to get out of the rain and wash her thick mop of curly hair.

John didn't change much either; for very brief periods he got low with the wet, like all of us; otherwise he tenaciously hung in there – rather like the knife-edge on his shorts and pants. It was noted, particularly by the other men, that the creases in his pants were always immaculate, whatever the conditions, and they asked if he had a trouser press in his tent? He hurried on to get into the warmth.

I hurried too. I was on my way to India! India the Antidote.

We all arrived at the camp, on a hillside overlooking Khandbari, in fine spirits; seeing in the far, far distance, across a crazy quilt of mountains, forests and terraces, Tumlingtar – and the landing field. Tomorrow Khandbari and its famed market!

The day dawned sunny. And bright and early, the morning air rang with Andy's strong Welsh voice, and Simon's prompting. 'There ain't nothing like a dame, nothing in the world, Ain't nothing quite the same that is anything like a dame . . . ' he sang, we sang. Pulling on our only clean T-shirts, dabbing on the perfume. 'Nothing cooks like a dame . . . ' patting the hair up at the sides; 'Nothing looks like a dame . . . ' glancing in the mirror briefly . . . 'Ain't nothing in this whole world . . . ' prancing about the camp in clumsy walking boots; ' . . . that is anything l-i-k-e . . . a dame . . . ' Khandbari, here we come!

Everyone, even the lads, were perfumed, and we sang happily in the sunshine as the tents came down in record time. We heaved on the backpacks, even patted the children's heads and waved goodbye to the mums watching us from their doorways. The elation was infectious, the pleasure doubled, the dog days gone – forgotten – as we skipped along the trail and merged into the growing hordes of villagers who poured down every artery of the mountains to go to market. Hundreds of villagers jostled in a colourful milling mass along the main highway – a vibrant, pulsating life force streaming into town. They carried their wares with them, chickens and eggs and potatoes and blankets and baskets and spice. And they chatted and laughed and smiled at us. It was a very special day, and nobody was enjoying it more than we were – the rain was gone – for good!

We started off in a tea-cum-beer house and sampled the lot: Indian gin, Indian whisky and beer. Walking through the streets to the market, we saw the earthquake damage – several houses partially or totally collapsed – and learnt in the ironmonger's that the monsoon had not only been the worst in living memory, but that it had flooded hundreds of acres in Bangladesh. Eight hundred people had died in Nepal alone, and it was only beaten by the 1934 earthquake when 8,500 died. That it had been bad, we knew – but the worst in fifty odd years! How did we manage to get that one? However, it was all gone now.

The market was a rich embroidery of life, providing by exchange, barter and sale a miscellany of basic merchandise. Bryan and Peter bought the locally-made *kukri* (knives), a long-desired acquisition for them and we bought rugs and pots and hats and took lots of photos of the umbrella maker, the candlestick maker, the carpets and camels, and chatted to anyone who'd talk to us. Some asked us to take photographs of them. One man particularly wanted his photograph taken with his ageing mother. He gave us his address and asked us to send him the picture. We were only too glad to do it, and wondered if in years to come he would cling to that picture, as it might be the only one he had of her. Later in the day, Susie and Joan visited the hospital, taking a small collection from us and seeing the patients.

On this, the penultimate night, we had our first ever evening meal outside, in balmy conditions. Because of the warm sultry night it took on ambrosial qualities, and we got a bit merry – because we'd been through merry hell we said. The lads thought we'd all displayed a level of endurance that would qualify us for the SAS. In that case we had come a long way, I thought. Now we discovered that Simon knew every word to every single Gilbert and Sullivan operetta you'd never wanted to hear. What a pity it took twenty-four days to find this out! When we went to bed Susie said, 'Wasn't that a lovely day?'

'Yes – a lovely day – perfect, in fact, and the last one will be the same.'

We played all the way down to Tumlingtar, and as we stood on a bluff overlooking the village and the landing field, we remarked again what a lovely day it had been, and how glad we were that the rain was all over. The last evening would just round off the whole trip nicely.

Dorjee and Andy arranged a final celebration dinner. We washed and polished ourselves up, rested and prepared for the last fling, looking forward to supper out on the grass.

But just before dinner it started to rain! We couldn't believe our bad luck. We slunk back to the mess tent, but we were relaxed despite the weather, now that we were away from the real horrors. Throughout the excellent meal we relived the trip's highlights, which had become almost legendary in our minds by now, but nothing could spoil our evening. We were laughing about something and Susie tossed her head back and put up her hand to brush her hair back – and let out a blood-curdling scream loaded with revulsion: 'Ugh! A leech – Oh God, I've got a leech in my hair!' The meal stopped. She shook her head violently, crying, 'Get it *out*!

All the latent horrors resurged – nerves tightened like violin strings. In a state of shock, we watched John separating her thick hair with fumbling fingers – trying to get at it. He poured on insect repellent and destroyed it for her – destroyed it for us, and then slimily pulled out a huge leech along the strands of her hair. We reeled, feeling nauseous. She mopped up the blood – and we decided to get out of the tent quick!

The cook-boys had a fire under their tarpaulin and as the rain was only fine drizzle we joined them. John fetched his song-book – we would enjoy ourselves no matter what!

The rain got worse; it began wetting the outside people and we moved farther in. John started the singing; the rain got heavier. We pressed farther in still and sang heartily. The wind blew, the candles spluttered, the fire lit up our faces roaring with song – and the rain beat the canvas. We sang louder, sang up, and the roof sagged with bowls of water, then overflowed in streams between us – and over us. I felt Helen nudge me. She was singing strongly and rolling her eyes as she pointed at her shoulder. The water streamed down her dangly earrings, over her shoulders and down her front. We nudged Susie to look! She laughed and stoically sang on.

John saw us looking at him, incredulity written on our faces – and he sang hard at us, punching the air. Come on, ignore the rain he was saying, beat it, don't let it get at us. And I thought, with a surge of pleasure as we shouted the words – what a team, what a crazy, crazy team! Down our necks and over our heads it poured, in a deluge from the roof, flowing now through every seam of the tent. Our hair stuck to our heads, our clothes stuck to our bodies, and we licked it off our faces. The porters, squatting down with their backs hunched up against it all, grinned on, dumbfounded by these insane people – all of us – the whole trekking group, drenched, and dementedly singing through a monsoon which would never leave us!

With the water pouring over my face I looked for him. I looked to the sky – and called out in anguish over the valiant choir and appalling rain: 'BEAR! – WHERE WERE YOU?'

Postscript

WHAT happened to the climbers? As so often in the Himalayas weather and snow conditions played a big part. The southwest face of Makalu proved too dangerous to attempt. Avalanches continually swept the face, and Doug decided to attempt the traditional route. Things had been going remarkably well and Rick Allen and Alan Hinckes were out in front and pushing for the summit. Rick was shortly due back in London and this was his last chance. They were roped together – joined by a Karabiner – when they came to a steep section which looked avalanche prone. Alan thought it was too dangerous – Rick wanted to go on a lead across when suddenly a loud crack rent the air and the whole slab started to move with Rick on it. Alan had a split second to decide – try to hold him, with the odds on being carried away very high, or unclip the rope, which he did. Rick fell some 1,500 feet and Alan looked down with horror on a bloodied mess in the snow. When Alan managed to reach him, Rick was in a poor state, but he patched him up and in a nine-hour epic Alan got him to a col where a doctor from the Spanish team attended to him. Doug and other team members eventually reached him and got him to the base camp. This effectively ended the assault on the mountain. Rick was taken out by helicopter and was then bitten by a mosquito at a refuelling stop and finished in hospital in Aberdeen with malaria and bigger problems than broken bones.